The Buck
Stops Here

THE EXECUTIVE'S GUIDE TO BOTTOM-LINE
DECISIONS AND ACTIONS

The Buck Stops Here

THE EXECUTIVE'S GUIDE TO BOTTOM-LINE DECISIONS AND ACTIONS

CARL HEYEL

VNR VAN NOSTRAND REINHOLD
NEW YORK

Copyright © 1994 by Van Nostrand Reinhold

Library of Congress Catalog Card Number 93-12895
ISBN 0-442-01721-9

I(T)P Van Nostrand Reinhold is an International Thomson Publishing Company. ITP logo is a trademark under license.

Printed in the United States of America.

Van Nostrand Reinhold   ITP Germany
115 Fifth Avenue   Königswinterer Str. 418
New York, New York 10003   53227 Bonn
                                          Germany

International Thomson Publishing
Berkshire House, 168-173   International Thomson Publishing Asia
High Holborn   38 Kim Tian Rd., #0105
London WC1V7AA   Kim Tian Plaza
England   Singapore

Thomas Nelson Australia   International Thomson Publishing Japan
102 Dodds Street   Kyowa Building, 3F
South Melbourne 3205   2-2-1 Hirakawacho
Victoria, Australia   Chiyada-Ku, Tokyo 102
                                          Japan

Nelson Canada
1120 Birchmount Road
Scarborough, Ontario
M1K 5G4, Canada

16 15 14 13 12 11 10 9 8 7 6 5 4 3 2 1

Library of Congress Cataloging-in-Publication Data

Heyel, Carl, 1908-
    The buck stops here : the executive's guide to bottom-line
decisions and actions / Carl Heyel.
      p. cm.
    Includes index.
    ISBN 0-442-01721-9
    1. Decision-making.   I. Title.
HD30.23.H49 1993
658.4'03—dc20   93-12895
                                                           CIP

To Rebecca Wang

The word *buck* has many meanings. One of them is colloquialism for the American Old West: short for a buck-horn handled knife. In poker games, the buck was any inanimate object (originally it was the knife) that was thrown into a jackpot and temporarily taken by the winner of the pot. Whenever the deal reached the holder of the buck, a new jackpot had to be made, i.e., the buck could not be passed any farther.

The buck stops here was a favorite phrase of President Harry S. Truman, who liked to use it whenever a matter on which a decision had to be made came before him. "On my desk," he wrote, "I have a motto which says 'The buck stops here'— meaning a decision has to be made, and I'm the one who has to make it."

Contents

Foreword | xi

What This Book Is About | xvii

Definitions and Clarifications | 1

Basic Propositions | 3

Category One: The Moment of Truth | 17

Category Two: Sizing Up | 25

Category Three: Marshaling the Evidence | 37

Category Four: Weighing the Evidence | 45

Category Five: Fallout | 57

Category Six: Under the Gun—The Final Act
of Decision | 67

Category Seven: Implementation | 73

Who Shall Make the Value Judgements? | 89

Appendix A: Are You Prepared for
Emergencies? | 97

Appendix B: Are You Prepared for
Crisis Management? | 103

Appendix C: Case Example:
Crisis Communications | 111

Index | 117

Foreword

There was a time when the gut-feeling, hunch-following, tycoon boss played center stage in business management from start to finish. This intuitive manager who dominated 19th century business saw industry as something he created—a grand product of his own genius. And, if he had talent, shrewdness, and a keen business sense, his intuitions were often more sound and far-sighted than those of his expert advisors.

With the rise of bigger and more complex organizations, however, this old-style decision maker lost ground. Few, if any, large corporations today confer that kind of authority on one person. Business decisions are no longer products of single-handed thinking. Usually they are made in the context of highly processed information and recommendations that flow from all levels of command in the organization. Indeed, these decisions must take into account what committees, boards of directors, shareholders, consumers, and even governments have to say. This means that there is far less room for the old-style, "flash-type," autocratic thinking of the past. What is needed instead is a mode of thinking in which the *justification* or *rational basis* for any decision is more or less explicitly articulated and available to all concerned, so that it can be shared as a basis for deliberation and possible consensus. Therefore, genuine *reasoning* and not raw gut feeling or flash intuition is required.

One result of all the complexity and technology in modern business thinking is the tendency of writers on management to see the business leader as a "model maker"—a model maker who believes that the best way to characterize the world is to represent it or, as we now say, *simulate* it, with a mathematical model. The heroes of this model maker are, of course, the scientists and technologists who, he believes, truly understand reality and shape it to their hearts' content.

Unfortunately, however, the model maker representation harbors some confusion between the hypothetical and the *actual* business manager. In this book, Carl Heyel clears up the matter. The business manager he describes is neither the intuitive autocrat of the past nor the model maker of the imagination. He is the real flesh and blood business leader of the present who, in the final analysis, makes his decisions in a manner that might be characterized as *quasi*-intuitive rather than simply "intuitive"—although, in this instance, logicians would most likely prefer to use the term, "informal" and drop "intuitive" altogether.

However informal the decision-making process may be, Heyel pointedly reminds us that, in its essential respects, this process calls for the observance of certain axiom-like "truths" which are basic to *all* decision making, for example: *mathematical analytical techniques may not be sufficient but this does not mean that they are not necessary; refusing to make a decision is tantamount to making one;* and, *decisions are judged by their consequences.* In addition to these "principles," Heyel offers a myriad of questions which a decision maker must not fail to ask herself/himself at the "moment of truth": *Are the excuses you have been advancing the true ones, or are you merely seeking to avoid some unpleasant consequences? Are you driven by a desire for unattainable (or unneeded) perfection? Are you fooling yourself about the time you have for coming to the decision?* The questions go on through several intriguing categories dealing with such crucial matters as: evidence—marshaling, selecting, and weighing it; fallout—in terms of repercussions, personal sacrifices, risk, ethics, and environment; final checks—regarding the decision maker's present state of mind, back-up from others, long and short-term considerations; implementation; . . .; and much more.

These are all mind stretching, soul searching, critical directives that call for solid reasoning and not mere intuiting. Nevertheless, the ultimately informal aspect of the process is what Heyel is stressing. The "real" decision maker must, in a final feat of intellect, fuse all reasoned results—as derived so far—with his own background of knowledge and experience. This final act *does* somewhat resemble old-fashioned intuition, but only because it is not explicitly mathematical, quantitative, or otherwise formal. Its rational basis, though perhaps somewhat implicit, is nonetheless essentially definable, and we can therefore characterize it as genuine reasoning, regardless of how informal it may be. The crucial distinction here is between formal and informal decision making;—this distinction closely parallels the distinction between formal and informal logic which has been so successfully drawn in our American colleges over the past decade or so.

The modern decision maker, the one presented by the author, is clearly of the informal sort.

In his final and especially intriguing chapter, Heyel takes up *value judgments* and the question of *who shall make them*. His remarkable structural analysis of how policy, and at least some of the over-all culture, of a business establishment is set is indeed a remarkable contribution, not to be missed by any corporate manager.

Mr. Heyel's graceful prose, taken literally, is a *prescriptive* account *par excellence*. It reads as an overall recommendation for *any* decision maker, industrial, political, personal, or other. More particularly and essentially, however, it is a *description* in the sense that it highlights the main features of *good* decision making as an informal process, and as good decision making essentially (and actually) occurs in modern business.

Contemporary literature on decision making of any sort features formal decision theory which has by now grown into an important and formidable branch of statistical analysis. It is time, however, that an author on business management as distinguished as this one returns to a consideration of what really transpires in the carpeted offices at the time of deliberation and choice. Our business executives are the highest paid employees in the world. Any authoritative account of what their decision and policy-making work is like, and of what it takes to carry it off, is naturally of immense potential interest not only to the principle actors, the executives themselves, but also to the shareholders, consumers, and citizens, who are affected by their decisions.

Carl Heyel's crisp and absorbing account will fascinate even the most casual reader.

S. Cannavo, Ph.D.,
Professor Emeritus,
Brooklyn College at the
    City University of New York
Adjunct Professor of Philosophy,
    Business and Liberal Arts
    Program, Queens College at the
    City University of New York

What This Book
Is About

This book is addressed to the person who, to use Harry Truman's memorable phrase, has to say, "The buck stops here!"

There are many books on executive decision making, but this book is different. Most such books give you logical and mathematical formulas designed to quantify the risks and payoffs of alternative courses of action. The tack this book takes is that such quantifications, helpful though they may be, actually represent the smallest part—perhaps no more than 10 percent—of the considerations that go into final choices and actions. The remaining 90 percent are the submerged but powerful influences of human frailties, preferences, passions, prejudices, fears, ambitions, pride, mendacity, chicanery—in short, the often undervalued and even unrecognized human ingredients.

The "management sciences" can tell you what proportion of different product options should make up the most economic manufacturing product mix for specific total sales projections, or how to reach "make or buy" decisions for product parts. But they won't tell you how to decide labor-relations issues, or how seriously to take air-pollution agitation, or how plant closings will affect employee motivation at ongoing operations, or how to gauge competitor moves or properly time product innovations. These are the kinds of decisions that are the burden of this book.

The intent of this book is not to make the decisions for you, but to make sure that you don't overlook or ignore any factors that should be weighed when you make the choices that will dictate your action. Here the sins of omission may outweigh any sins of commission: neglecting to take something important into account, or taking something for granted that should have been questioned. Or judgmental errors that can lead you astray, making a decision too soon and closing out options or vacillating too long and finding the horse gone when you decide to bolt the barn door. Or out of ignorance or misinformation or rashness, rushing in where angels would not have dared to tread.

Note that this is a workbook, not a read-through-and-put-on-the-shelf book. It calls for active participation by the reader. It poses questions that must be faced and answered in a rational process. The questions are definitely not rhetorical. They are offered as think-triggers, to help you analyze your attitudes and motivations and give proper attention to all of the subjective factors that must not be ignored when you make your final choice/decision and establish your line of action.

The operative words are *final choice/decision*. This book is concerned with what you do *after* your own preliminary investigations, *after* the recommendations by the experts, when you have to say, "Yes, let's do it," or "No, this is not for us (or for me)." When the chips are down, when the moment of truth has come and the time for action is at hand, do you buy the prescription as developed? Do you accept the conclusions of the professionals? Do you second-guess the experts? What do you do when the experts disagree? Or when the experts merely give pros and cons and drop the hot potato back into your lap? Or what if you have no experts to advise you, and you made all of the analyses yourself? How sure are you of your own findings? Have you missed anything?

A "canny operator" may be able to say yes or no as soon as the pros and cons are laid on the table. Another, more methodical decision maker may want more time for reflection and double-checking. In both cases sound decision making is a highly complex matter—a parading before the mind's eye of alternative moves and chains of consequences, and an alertness to caveats.

The process is the same in both cases—only the decision makers are different. The one known for making sound decisions quickly is actually going through an elaborate series of weighings and balancings at a faster pace by virtue of a long memory of similar situations and by a knack of quickly perceiving patterns of relationships.

That's what executive responsibility is all about— making decisions. Not doing. Functional operatives and departments do that. *Executive* action consists in determining what the functional people and departments are to do. The job of the person with final responsibility is to decide *what* is to be done, *when* it is to be done, and xx | The Buck Stops Here

in large measure *who* is to do it. The *why* has been part of the decision-making process. Basically, the *who, how,* and *where* are up to those charged with the doing.

The intent here is to make an in-depth dissection that will uncover for examination, to the extent possible, all conceivable kinds of decision. Obviously, this will result in no small list. Different components will apply with differing emphasis to specific cases, and in many cases not at all. And, of course, it is not suggested that in practice, especially in emergency situations, every choice will proceed by taking time out for methodically checking every item on the list and carefully weighing those that apply. The process must always be more automatic and much faster than that.

The point to be made now is that the automatic process, in too many instances, overlooks or gives insufficient weight to all relevant options and consequences, because doing so has not become an habitual pattern of thinking. The result is a poor decision, or a "not-best" decision. This book's premise is that taking time out to analyze decision making in the abstract, developing an all-embracing model without regard to specifics, will provide the necessary "mental set" that will make the automatic process for real choices efficient and effective.

The model consists of 270 questions and commentary, organized into the following seven categories:

1. The Moment of Truth

2. Sizing Up

3. Marshaling the Evidence

4. Weighing the Evidence

5. Fallout

6. Under the Gun: The Final Act of Decision

7. Implementation

Succeeding chapters take up each one of the above categories in turn. The chapter immediately following lays the groundwork by developing the basic propositions upon which decision-making analysis must rest.

A point to be emphasized ties in with the remarks made earlier about final choice/decision coming after preliminary investigations and recommendations. This book's model does not include the mathematical analyses that are such a prominent part of most books on decision theory. Based on research for military operations in World War II, quantitative techniques—operations research, linear programming, dynamic programming, game theory, and others—have been developed and refined to provide a rational, scientific basis for management decisions. Additionally, there has been great interest in so-called decision support systems, by which, with appropriate software, individual executives can rapidly quantify alternative proposed actions before arriving at strategies and decisions in their fields.

It is to be reiterated that the results of these techniques are considered here to be only the preliminaries to ultimate choices. The final choices must be made by human beings and not by computer printouts or mathematical formulas. Even if a purportedly airtight set of findings based on quantitative analysis were presented to you, you could still not safely make a decision by simply opting for the action that the analysis "proved" would provide the best bottom line. Decisions by the executive with the-buck-stops-here responsibility are not that simple.

Definitions and Clarifications

There is a close and overlapping relationship among the terms *choice*, *selection*, *decision*, and *value judgments*. All involve considerations of alternatives, and, presumably, action or calls for action. For the present purposes, this book makes the following demarcations:

Choice here is the marshaling and weighing of information concerning alternatives, with the objective of arriving at a single preferred course of action, or at least a hierarchy of preferences.

Selection is the mental act of identifying the preference to oneself, perhaps accompanied by the physical act of pointing to or touching or picking up something. Choice is conceived of as a process, with selection as its end result.

Decision is the final act of solidifying the selection and formulating it in words for necessary promulgation and translation into action.

Value judgment herein means the mental approach brought to bear on the choices that precede decision—dictated by ingrained professional training, cultural background, moral guidelines, ethical standards, and the like. These influences, of course, also help to shape the goals to which the choice/decision process is directed. Value judgments go a long way in "prefabricating" some kinds of decisions as foregone conclusions, making them "not negotiable"—a result that makes the periodic examination of values of prime importance.

The *choice/decision process* is a series of steps designed to culminate in an action to resolve the stressful situation that arises when, to achieve certain objectives or to avoid certain undesirable or harmful eventualities, it has become evident that some action must be taken, but that in some cases various conflicting actions are possible.

Basic Propositions

THE LOGIC UNDERLYING ANALYSIS OF
DECISION MAKING

**1. MATHEMATICAL ANALYTICAL TECHNIQUES ARE
NOT TO BE DENIGRATED.** Focusing on the unquantifiable emotional, predilective, and other subjective factors in the choice/decision process does not entail downgrading the applicability of statistical analysis and other mathematical techniques for optimization. Stating that they are not sufficient does not mean that they are unnecessary, but it does mean that two caveats are in order:

a. There should be an awareness of the problematic and probabilistic assumptions underlying the mathematical formulations, so that the decision maker or recommender is not misled by the cloak of seeming precision often unsupportably bestowed upon mathematically stated results.

b. In the business setting, the appropriate relative emphasis to place on mathematical analysis and its implications is often a matter of sheer personal opinion at some authorization level. It is in the formulation of these opinions and their culmination in decisions that the unquantifiable subjective factors play their overriding part.

2. THE FINAL ACT OF DECISION ALWAYS RESULTS IN RELIEVING THE TENSION AND ANXIETY OF WEIGHING CONFLICTING ALTERNATIVES DURING THE PROCESS OF CHOICE. During the period of emotional stress, the decision maker yearns for a return to the "sentiment of rationality" which the psychologist William James has described as a strong feeling of ease, peace, and rest.

3. THE SENTIMENT OF RATIONALITY IS NO SURE CRITERION OF A SOUND DECISION. The problem is that if the choice, because of ignorance or subconscious inclination, overlooks crucial considerations, the sentiment of rationality will be one of short-lived euphoria, something that the ill-informed and self-deluded person can readily achieve. The yearning for it accounts for the propensity to make snap judgments, on the premise that action—any action—is better than doing nothing.

There is one and only one prescription for the avoidance of false rationality, and that is to consider, within the constraints of time and available facilities, *all* conceivable factors influencing choice. Thus the sentiment of rationality must itself be tested, to be sure that the immediate relief at having made a choice is not spurious.

4. FREE WILL IS CIRCUMSCRIBED. The process of choice and the act of decision are far less subject to will than is commonly supposed. We think we act on our own volition, but are largely unconscious of what wills us to will as we do. Since Freud advanced his concepts of id, ego, and superego, there has come about a widespread recognition of conflicting tendencies and conflicting drives rooted in cultural and familial conditioning, in addition to biological urgings over which we have no or little free-will control. In more recent years, the findings of genetic and neurological research have further diminished the domain of free will: The genes bequeathed to us by our parents set definite parameters to our mental, emotional, and physical development, to the way we react to situations, to the way we think. And all of this is to say nothing of the powerful influence of the environment in which we live in our formative years.

But the foregoing does not mean that free will must abdicate completely to determinism. Despite all the encroachments indicated, there remains a still-powerful *kernel of consciousness* and locus of volition—the "I" of Descartes's "I think, therefore I am." Or call it the soul, the psyche, the mind, the self. This small kernel of consciousness bestows upon the decision maker a broad area of choice. The person who comes out short in the genetic, psychic, and environmental lottery can nevertheless surpass the decisional track record of his luckier but less diligent friend, by dint of more effective exploitation of the endowments he has, despite the constrictions upon the sovereignty of his free will.

COROLLARY: It is impossible to divorce decision making from emotions. However, there will be differences in the degree to which emotional factors influence final choice. The key to decisional success is awareness of one's innate propensities and limitations, so that they can consciously be compensated for.

5. ALL MORAL GUIDES FOR CHOICE, DECISION, AND ACTION BECOME SLIPPERY STANCHIONS WHEN NEEDED MOST. It is easy to subscribe to the Ten Commandments under the tolerable vicissitudes of routine existence, but in dire emergency situations we find them difficult to cling to. The most solemn of them—thou shalt not kill, thou shalt not commit adultery, thou shalt not steal, thou shalt not bear false witness, thou shalt not covet—are all quite readily rationalized away when mortal decision makers are confronted with terrifying dangers or threats or the strong beguilements of temptation: In time of war the gentlest man kills, and in peace will kill or condone the taking of life in self defense...Eros prevails and illicit lovers yield to the imperious demands of the flesh...With his children starving, the desperate man steals food...Before the cock crows twice, Peter's denials thrice bear witness against Christ....And many a smile and hypocritical word cloak covetousness and gnawing jealousy.

COROLLARY #1: When implementing a contemplated decision means relying upon the assumed reactions of others, as is almost always the case, a precautionary note is to be sounded: How certain or how probable is it that the pattern of past choices and actions of those involved in implementation are predictive of their actions under stresses flowing from the decision? How slippery are *their* moral stanchions?

COROLLARY #2: The contemplated decision may be the result of unconscious realization of moral shortfalls that the decision maker has been unwilling to face.

6. DECISIONS ARE JUDGED BY CONSEQUENCES. A decision is *correct* if, as a result of it, a predetermined objective to which the decision is germane is attained. A decision is *good* if the objective is good, i.e., has beneficent consequences. All good decisions are by definition correct ones, but a correct decision is not necessarily a good one. A *sound* decision will herein denote one that is either correct or good.

A decision may be sound even though its objectives are not attained, if the lack of attainment is due to failure in implementation. Therefore, in reaching a decision, the methods and practicality of implementation must be given the same attention as all other factors influencing choice.

A decision may be a bad decision if its consequences transgress moral or societal standards, but may still be a correct one if those consequences were a recognized part of the decision maker's objectives. The analysis of and techniques for sound decision making are equally applicable to good and bad objectives. The choice/decision process herein explicated is descriptive, not prescriptive.

> COROLLARY: Before the application of the rational choice/decision process, there must be a prior examination of objectives and goals. If these are detrimental to others or transgress the decision maker's normally adhered-to moral code, the process can still be pursued effectively if the decision maker admits that fact to himself. It need not be admitted publicly.

7. NO DECISION STANDS ALONE. All decisions are linked in time to the future events they influence, and in space to effects upon persons and projects not a direct part of the problem faced by the decision maker.

The connection may in fact be tenuous, but "no man is an island, entire of itself." Therefore, in weighing consequences, the decision maker must not overlook fallout.

8. AN ASPECT OF DECISION MAKING NOT TO BE OVERLOOKED IS THE EASE AND COST OF REVERSING THE DECISION IF IT IS LATER PROVED WRONG.

COROLLARY: The decision-implementation linkage thus calls for ensuring adequate feedback and the establishment of appropriate checkpoints.

9. EFFECTIVE DECISIONS REQUIRE BENCHMARKS FOR CONSISTENCY. Ironclad consistency is not a requirement for building a track record of sound decisions. But traveling without benefit of benchmarks and guidelines is hazardous. Confidence in facing unknown choices in the future can be enhanced by a strong core of beliefs, or a "mental set" against which to measure contemplated actions.

The benchmarks will consist of moral and ethical standards based on early upbringing, religious teachings, continuing education, and purposeful thought. With such fortification, the decision maker can without hesitation dismiss many options out of hand. He[1] does not relinquish volition, because the "kernel of consciousness" can, after due deliberation, make an exception, but previously set standards will not be breached by default. (Note that no previously set standards will last indefinitely or perhaps even for very

[1]Throughout our text, the masculine pronoun in locutions such as this one will be understood to include both genders. Where only the masculine gender is intended, the text will make that clear.

long. For example, changing mores lead to reinterpretation of even divinely established commandments and taboos.)

10. A CONFLICT BETWEEN A PROPOSED DECISION AND A BASIC CORE OF BELIEFS CALLS FOR AN IMMEDIATE PRELIMINARY DECISION BEFORE INITIATING THE CHOICE/DECISION PROCESS. As previously indicated, if the objectives and/or readily seen by-products of the actions being considered are entertained even if they infract previously held moral and ethical standards, the decision can still be a correct one (although not necessarily a good one) if it passes all of the pertinent choice/decision tests. However, the decision maker must expect a feeling of unease and a gnawing at his self-esteem—the manifestations of a guilty conscience.

11. CONSCIENCE CANNOT BE COMPLETELY RELIED UPON TO PROVIDE POSITIVE INSTRUCTIONS. Conscience, as Immanuel Kant pointed out, is an instinct to pass judgment upon ourselves in accordance with moral law. It is not a faculty that we can apply as we wish; it is an inner voice that comes to us unbidden. Its reproaches can for a time be stifled, but not completely or for an indefinite length of time. Even if submerged in our subconscious, conscience exacts its toll.

However, note that in the choice/decision process, conscience as a rule only prods us *against* a contemplated act, or brings out its nagging tones *after* a wrong deed has been done. Thus it cannot be relied upon by the decision maker to provide positive instructions. Since not flashing a red light is not the same as flashing a green light, the decision maker must go through the choice/decision steps to ensure a robust and enduring sentiment of rationality.

12. ONE USEFUL WAY TO CATEGORIZE DECISIONS IS TO DO SO UNDER THREE HEADINGS: PERSONAL, SURRO-GATE, AND GROUP. *Personal* decisions have to do with the decision maker's personal future or the futures of his family and others for whom he holds responsibility, accepted or imposed. He is the final authority for the decisions, responsible for initiating and perhaps supervising implementation, and, to a major degree, for the outcome.

Surrogate decisions have to do with decisions made in an executive or administrative capacity for an organization such as a business, a community group or public body, or a church. Here, while the decision maker assumes responsibility for his decisions and stakes his relationship with his organization on their soundness in the long run, the legal responsibility for the resulting actions is shared with the organization, and does not rest solely with him.

Group decisions are those for which the decision maker is a chairman or member of a governing body, such as a board of directors or board of trustees, or is a member of committees of various kinds. Here the responsibility for the decision and resulting actions is the work of a specially created entity, and personal responsibility and usually financial liability are diluted. Decisions are properly group decisions if they have to do with broad policy matters as distinguished from administrative actions. Their areas of responsibilities are spelled out in constitutions, charters, bylaws, and the like.

Committees and business-conference groups are useful for the joint consideration of certain problems by persons qualified to have an opinion. But note that they cannot "do" anything. They can only *analyze, formulate*, and *recommend*. They are not viable substitutes for executive action.

13. REFUSING TO MAKE A DECISION IS TANTAMOUNT TO MAKING A DECISION. Making no decision is, by default, a decision to relinquish whatever opportunity exists in the situation for the decision maker to exercise volition. It is at best a decision to leave the outcome to blind chance, and at worst a decision to submit to unfavorable forces that might otherwise be controlled or curtailed.

COROLLARY #1: It is not necessarily true that making some kind of decision is better than making no decision at all, despite the fact that this admonition is frequently heard. Making a bad snap decision can in fact have more harmful results than allowing blind chance or uncontrolled hostile forces to have their way. The point is that a "do-nothing" decision must rest upon the same kind of choice/decision procedure as does a positive decision.

COROLLARY #2. The postponement of a decision, if analysis shows that additional time is available, is preferable to a quick decision devoid of the sentiment of rationality, provided the extra time is given to purposeful thought. But postponement can allow a decision maker to slip into procrastination, which can soon lead to making excuses for not acting.

COROLLARY #3. Another pitfall is deciding upon half- measures in order to stave off facing the need for a more unpleasant decision, which will have to be faced sooner or later anyway. Here wishful thinking—the hope that something more pleasing will turn up—must be guarded against.

COROLLARY #4. Still another pitfall is the temptation to fall back upon a group decision when the matter is one for forthright action by the responsible executive.

14. AN UNENFORCEABLE OR LOGICALLY UNWORKABLE DECISION IS NOT A "REAL" DECISION. Examples: Napoleon's "paper blockade"...the tale of the mice deciding to pin the bell on the cat ...issuing work rules that go against culturally ingrained habits...giving leadership decrees without a base of followership.

15. A DECISION, EVEN THOUGH THEORETICALLY WORKABLE, THAT DOES NOT RESULT IN ACTION, IS NOT A "REAL" DECISION. Without subjecting the decision to a test, it is impossible to say whether the decision was good or bad. It is neither, and so it is nothing. The choice/decision process calls for a continuing awareness of the linkage between a decision and expectable recipient reactions, covering cultural, economic, health, and emotional factors.

16. CRITERIA FOR DECISION MAKING WILL NOT BE IDENTICAL IN DIFFERING DECISION MILIEUS. Two decision makers, each having conscientiously followed the choice/decision model presented herein and applying it to identical objectives, can arrive at entirely different, but in each case sound, decisions. The results will be influenced by the following:

a. The locus of the action to be taken as a result of the decision may lie within totally different cultures, economic environment, and political systems, creating differing problems of implementation and differing standards of social acceptability.

b. The surrounding conditions facing the two decision makers will point to differing fallouts. (Cf. Proposition 7.)

c. The "mental set" (cf. Proposition 9) may be widely different, resulting in different cores of belief by which each will judge the contemplated decision.

d. Differing facilities for implementation will lead to widely differing feasibility judgments.

17. THE DIFFERING DECISIONS REFERRED TO IN PROPOSITION 16 MAY PRESAGE ACTIONS THAT ARE MUTUALLY HARMFUL OR DANGEROUS. Following are important possible eventualities:

a. The resources and facilities of one decision maker may so greatly predominate over those of others that he can confront the others with a *force majeure* and make his decision prevail.

b. Through negotiation, joint decisions acceptable to all can be reached, resolving the conflict.

c. No decision to ameliorate the conflict will be taken. This under the best scenario results in postponement until the time when (b) can be accomplished—or adversely, (cf. Proposition 13) it leaves the outcome to possible disastrous chance, or to an adverse balance of power.

d. In frustration because of no forward movement in negotiations, one of the decision makers opts for the "arbitrament of force." This may end in victory by one, or in a stalemate. If the latter, it may lead to a reversion to (c) after futile sacrifices.

e. In frustration because of no forward movement in negotiations, one of the decision makers makes the unpalatable decision to be the first to make a concession.

18. TWO ADVERSE FACTORS ARE OPERATIVE IN LARGE-ORGANIZATION DECISION MAKING. They are:

a. Loss of realism because of the distance between the decision maker and the scene of the specified action.

b. The dangers inherent in the fact that decision makers in the thick of things are not in position to see the big picture. Where the problem is one of too many organizational layers between the formulators of decisions at the top and their implementation at operational levels, the following corrective formula can be applied, enunciated in an early paper by Harold F. Smiddy, a vice-president of General Electric.

> The determinant level for responsibility and authority to make a particular decision should be at the lowest organization level where both the needed skills and competence on the one hand, and the needed information—embracing understanding of both indirect and environmental probable impacts of the decision—on the other hand, can reasonably be brought to exist.

19. "DAMNED IF YOU DO, DAMNED IF YOU DON'T" SITUATIONS: Here doing A or not doing A will result in possibly irreparable harm or violate one or more strongly held moral standards. The only option is to make the decision that will apparently cause the least harm. If this cannot be determined, the decision maker can only underscore his acceptance of responsibility by openly opting for A or B, and making clear his assessment of the alternatives.

> **COROLLARY:** The fact of life that emerges from the above is that *some problems have no solution.*

However, this notion should be entertained only as a very last resort, after all rational approaches have been exhausted.

20. THE MOST IMPORTANT BY-PRODUCT OF SOUND DE-CISION MAKING IS THAT IT FORESTALLS POSTDECISIO-NAL REGRET. Such regret intrudes even if forces beyond the decision maker's control preclude the attainment of the sought-after result.

The following chapters discuss the categories of things a sound decision maker—you—should think about.

CATEGORY ONE
The Moment of Truth

moment of truth: *the time of the final sword-thrust in a bull-fight* (Sp. el momento de la verdad); transf., *a crisis or turning point; a testing situation.*

—*Oxford English Dictionary*

The crisis or turning point, the testing situation which all of us, like the matador, must face *alone*, comes before the final decision that culminates in action. It is the decision to make a decision, the recognition that this is the end of the third tercio of the bullfight, the time for the final sword thrust.

Many are the causes, admitted or not, of the reluctance or inability to face the moment of truth. The enemies inside the gates are vacillation, laziness, ignorance, self-deception, cowardice, obduracy, and a host of others. These forces of darkness and denial can be exorcised only by bringing them into the light. That is what you will do with the help of the following questions.

NOTE: It will be seen that many of the self-check questions herein and in succeeding chapters thrust in opposing directions—in one case seeking to make sure that no pertinent factors are overlooked, and in another case cautioning against too much analysis; in one case inveighing against procrastination and vacillation, in another warning against snap judgments. But that is the way the real world impacts you, with conflicting pushes and pulls. *You* have to do the selecting and *you* have to bear the responsibility for the consequences. "You pays your money and you makes your choice" is turned around: "You makes your choice, and *then* you pays your money."

1. ARE THE EXCUSES YOU HAVE BEEN ADVANCING TO YOURSELF AND TO OTHERS THE TRUE ONES—OR ARE YOU MERELY SEEKING TO AVOID SOME SELF-CENTERED UNPLEASANT CONSEQUENCES? In high-level positions in the business world this can be extremely costly, like continuing with an unprofitable product line or an obsolete plant instead of cutting losses. In middle management, a most frequent instance is the shoring up of incompetent subordinates.

Related to the above is addressing symptoms rather than the real underlying problem. Symptoms are always easier to treat, because palliatives will bring low-cost, low-pain temporary relief, but it is deceptive relief because the basic malfunction will worsen. The subtle problem here is unconscious self-deception—unconscious, that is, to surface thinking, but nevertheless known deep down. You refuse to admit to yourself that you are aware of the real problem because tackling it NOW will be painful.

2. IS THE FEAR OF "LOSS OF FACE" KEEPING YOU FROM WANTING TO ANNOUNCE A DECISION? It may be that the decision in question would mean a reversal of a previous stand you had taken. This may entail some discomfiture, but the common tendency is to exaggerate the degree to which others will judge the reversal in your personal terms. Are you obscuring the benefits of the right decision because of pride which may have no basis in fact? You may (with justification) be the center of your own universe, but you are definitely not the center of theirs! Rather than thinking disparagingly of you, the chances are that others are not spending a great deal of time thinking about you at all.

3. ARE YOU PLAYING THE ROLE OF CHARLES DICKENS' MR. MICAWBER? The character in *David Copperfield* always put off facing the hard facts of life in his fond expectation that "something will turn up," or that the problem calling for decision and action would go away, like an unwelcome guest. How many a visit to the doctor or dentist has been put off by that fond hope? How many a needed business or political decision delayed?

No planning is complete without hope, and, indeed, without the balm of hope few of us could face life's vicissitudes. But hope alone, without decision and resolute action, remains an unpredictable friend.

4. ARE YOU HOLDING OFF IN THE HOPE OF DILUTING A DECISION THAT IS PROPERLY YOURS? In the business arena, at some executive levels, a favorite tactic is to try to substitute a committee or group recommendation for something a single executive should decide on his own. (Cf. Proposition 12.) Lee Iacocca makes the point succinctly in his autobiography: "Most important decisions in corporate life are made by individuals, not by committees."

5. ARE YOU DRIVEN BY A DESIRE FOR UNATTAINABLE (OR UNNEEDED) PERFECTION? In business decisions having to do with product development, the failure to distinguish between what is "commercially right" and the "ultimate" in design or function will usually mean that a competitor runs off with the market while the company striving for too high an approach to perfection is left at the starting gate. Similarly, other kinds of decisions may be held off while the decision maker seeks ever more and more market or economic data or laboratory test results before taking the plunge.

6. ARE YOU FOOLING YOURSELF ABOUT THE TIME YOU HAVE FOR COMING TO THE DECISION? This is a devilishly effective form of self-deception. Old-movie buffs will remember Vivien Leigh as Scarlett O'Hara in *Gone with the Wind*. When contemplating the need to confront an uncomfortable situation, she would shrug off the unwelcome thought by saying, "I'll worry about that tomorrow." Most of us tend on occasion to soothe ourselves with the same lullaby, using expressions that recognize the gravity of the choice confronting us, but letting the exact moment of truth dangle in a comforting vagueness: "We'll have to do something about that *before too long*"; "I'll have to clean up that situation *one of these days*"..."Just put it on the VISA card." (There's a nice time lag in the credit-card system.)

You can "buy time" by such stavings-off, but you have to pay interest. The little gnawing sense of uneasiness never entirely leaves you, and when the day of reckoning arrives, the size of the reckoning comes as a shock.

7. ARE YOU SIMPLY BLOCKING OUT THE UNPALATABLE? We are all prone to think about the unthinkable as briefly and as infrequently as possible. How often do you feel inclined to contemplate your own death? Perhaps when an insurance salesman has you cornered and gets your signature—albeit having carefully euphemized the ugly word into "if anything happens to you" or "if your family were ever faced with the need to provide for themselves." Lawyers drawing up your will are also masters of circumlocution: "When this will becomes effective" or "Upon the trustees assuming their responsibilities."

But there will come times when you must grit your teeth and think about the unthinkable.

NOTE: All of the above is not to deny the benefits of being able to turn off some thoughts until their need arises; otherwise we could not exist at all. Nepenthe, in proper dosage, can be an effective therapeutic drug. But the kernel of consciousness must be in charge.

8. ARE YOU FUDGING THE ISSUE BY SUBSTITUTING HALF-MEASURES RATHER THAN FACING THE ISSUE HEAD ON? A business situation in point may involve the costly continuation of an unprofitable product line when there may be insufficient funds to do the really all-out advertising and promotional job called for. Vacillation will result in spending just enough to keep the product alive, but never enough to restore the viability of the line. Aside from the profit drain of preventing full exploitation of other lines, the amount of executive time and energy expended on the limping product is out of all proportion to the results. Company and personal prestige, vanity, hope that something will turn up—all combine to create a reluctance to face the decision to cut.

9. ARE YOU OVERLOOKING SOME INTERMEDIATE DECISIONS THAT CAN ENABLE YOU TO PLAY FOR TIME CONSTRUCTIVELY? The operative word here is *constructively.* There must be a commitment to use the time gained for purposeful thought, not for continued vacillation. And, of course, the intermediate actions contemplated are not to be the half-measures covered in the preceding question.

If action in a situation is bogged down by indecision, the ring of vacillation may be broken by stepping back and making a reevaluation of all aspects, to see if intermediate measures are available. The important point is to prevent indecision and inaction from merging imperceptibly into default by no decision. (Cf. Proposition 13.)

10. ARE YOU COURTING ANALYSIS PARALYSIS? How can you tell when to stop seeking more information? You can't—precisely. No analysis will ever provide *all* pertinent information. Intuition and time and cost constraints are all that will determine when the search should end. There always comes a time when the hand as dealt must be played, or the cards laid down. What is the risk in further delay? Has the problem been sufficiently sized up? (This point is further developed in Category Two, "Sizing Up.")

11. ARE YOU ALLOWING YOURSELF TO BE CONFUSED BY EXPERTS? President Franklin D. Roosevelt once plaintively commented that what he really needed were some one-armed economists. The ones he had, he complained, were too prone to present a detailed analysis pointing to actions in one direction, only to follow with "on the other hand" arguments pointing in the opposite direction. We can empathize with FDR's complaint, but in this high-tech age, the public-administration general-

ist cannot hope to base his decisions on his own knowledge. As Harlan Cleveland has put it, what you need to know in order to act knowingly expands much faster than your ability to absorb new knowledge. The obvious escape from this dilemma, he says, is not to learn more about the details of whatever it is, but to learn more about its *context*.

Learning about the context means weighing the knowledge-based information presented by the experts against the perspective of the larger picture into which it must be fitted. (This point is made here as an alert—it is discussed in detail under Category Four, "Weighing the Evidence.")

12. ARE YOU BEING NIBBLED TO DEATH BY MICE? Are you distracted by so many minor problems that you have insufficient time for the really important issues requiring your attention? Maybe the problem is lack of delegation. Maybe you need an assistant—but before saying that, it will be a good idea to consider whether some of the following emotional blocks account for your problem:

> **a.** Are you suffering from a gnawing feeling of insecurity? This often happens when a younger executive is newly appointed to a responsible post. He is painfully aware that he knows less on any subject than some key member of his staff, and to compensate he gets himself more and more immersed in details in the hope of becoming independent of his subordinates—an impossibility.
>
> **b.** Do you lack confidence in the ability of others to do their jobs? Is this an ego-centered rationalization? There are executives whose egos demand that they surround themselves with lesser lights, so that they themselves will shine more brightly.

c. Are you reluctant to admit, even to yourself, that someone knows more than you do? This is akin to (a) above, but there is a basic difference: the motivation here is not so much fear as conceit.

d. Are you afraid of not getting credit? Here again a fundamental insecurity manifests itself.

e. Are you afraid of a subordinate's moving ahead too fast? This may happen (1) where an executive approaching retirement is afraid of implying that he is slipping; and (2) where there is not a significant span between the ages of a relatively young executive and an able and ambitious subordinate.

f. Is there a problem of softness—a basic fear of conflict? There may be such a strong desire to be well liked that the result is lack of firmness in demanding that subordinates carry their proper load.

Recognizing the above causes of ineffectiveness for what they are will be the first and necessary step in exorcising them.

CATEGORY TWO

Sizing Up

You've got to develop a talent for perspective. Bernard Baruch once defined this as the ability to walk around a big problem the way a photographer walks around a subject he's going to photograph, saying nothing, mulling things over. Finally he says, "We'll take it from this angle."

A lot of questions have to be asked to apply Mr. Baruch's "talent for perspective" in sizing up a choice/decision situation. Let's get specific:

1. SHOULD YOU BE MAKING THIS DECISION AT ALL? Is it somebody else's baby? What cutoff point, if any, have you established to determine the types of problems that require your special, personal attention? If the cutoff point is too low, you're not as good a manager as you can be.

The cutoff point will, of course, vary for different jobs. For example, at one level an executive may not be concerned with any matter that involves less than, say, $100,000. For another executive or department head it might be $10,000, and for a section head, $2,500. A high-level policy executive may not be concerned with *any* current problem at all.

2. IS THIS A CRISIS SITUATION? Obviously, if there is a fire outside your office door, the immediate action called for—to put out the blaze or leave the scene—leaves little room for reflection and weighing of pros and cons. Reaction must be immediate and instinctive, and no advice to guide your response *during* the emergency is offered here. And that goes for immediate-action emergencies all the way up from wastebasket fires to disasters. However, *after* any serious emergency it will be well to hold a post mortem by yourself or with others, to—

Prevent recurrence through proper precautionary measures, training, and physical safeguards.

Assure orderly procedures during future emergencies, by means of proper operating procedures, fixed responsibilities, and periodic drills.

The crisis choices and decisions we refer to here are not those made in the midst of accident or disaster. Organizational steps that must be taken to assure readiness to cope effectively with such eventualities require a book of their own. The "crisis situation" addressed here concerns such matters as a deteriorating job situation in which your possible severance looms, or the results of a series of mistakes or questionable judgments on your part which are about to catch up with you, or how to adjust to the not-to-be-camouflaged failure of a project for which you were responsible.

It is obvious that corrective action or damage control is called for, since by now it is clear that taking no action presages intolerable consequences. Fortunately, the chances are that the matter is not entirely out of your hands, and there is still time for purposeful thought. Here are some basic prescriptions:

a. Don't panic. Easier said than done, of course, but it must be done. Take a look at Webster's definition:

> **panic:** a sudden, overpowering fright; espec., a sudden groundless fright; terror inspired by a trifling cause or a misapprehension of danger, especially when accompanied by unreasoning or frantic efforts to secure safety.

Pay special attention to the operative words *sudden and groundless, trifling cause, misapprehension of danger.* Think hard about them now, so that they will automatically come to mind when the emergency is upon you. Don't jump to the conclusion that available escape routes are closed. Make a considered effort to think of all possible alternatives calmly, and to evaluate them objectively.

b. Recognize the justification for fear, but assume a calm and confident air. That will help calm those who look to you for leadership. Nervousness is contagious, but so is calm determination.

c. Think of the worst scenario and start putting together ideas about how the worst effects can be dampened, what can be salvaged, what kinds of help are available.

d. Keep your plight in perspective. Lowell Thomas tells of a time when he was truly at low ebb: out of a job, practically broke, and nothing in sight. He was even concerned about where he would get his next pair of shoes. Then he passed a man hobbling along on crutches—because he had no feet. "Here I am," he told himself, "worrying about not having shoes, when that fellow doesn't even have any feet!"

e. Avail yourself of whatever strength your particular religious beliefs may bestow. There may be room for philosophic skepticism, but there is no doubt about the psychological efficacy for the believer of "If God be for me, who can be against me?"

3. WHAT IS THE MAGNITUDE OF THE DECISION? In a business situation, how much money is at risk to do the job right? For immediate requirements, and later? Will funding present difficulties? If the sums are large in terms of ordinary operations, what other resources can be explored?

How serious are the factors other than monetary? In business, for example, consider public relations...customer relations...prestige. In personal matters, bear in mind effect on career...family preferences...professional standing.

How confident are you that you are not over your head in this matter. If you are, are you ready to admit it—to yourself? To others? What options are available to shore up your endeavors? Or should you bow out rather than undertake the chance of falling on your face?

4. WHAT IS THE TRUE RANGE OF THE CHOICE/DECISION PROBLEM CONFRONTING YOU? It may be broader than you at first thought, and realizing this may lead you to a different concept of objectives and approach. Successful advertisers and marketers have long recognized the tremendous advantage of basing product design and marketing decisions on thinking about objectives in the broadest possible terms. The following point is made by marketing expert Lee Adler:

> To classify customer requirements, we have to think not only of function and economic product roles, but of psychological, situational, symbolic, religious, familial, and other intangible product benefits…. *What is the customer really buying?* Customers do not buy *food*: they buy nutrition, good taste, social status, ceremony, time saving, and many other benefits. Consumers do not buy *fuel oil*: they buy warmth and good health. They do not buy *insurance*: they buy anxiety reduction.

5. SHOULD THE RANGE OF DECISIONS BE NARROWED, SIMPLIFYING THE CHOICE/DECISION PROCESS? This would appear to contradict the thrust of the preceding question. However, the purpose here is to point out that there may be good reasons for breaking a complex decisional problem into logical subproblems. These can be prioritized, and the most important or most pressing ones tackled first. The purpose is not to deprecate broadening the overall objective, but to make breakdowns for methodical attack.

6. WHAT ARE THE "POLITICS" OF THE DECISION? "Politics," said Prince Otto von Bismarck, "is the doctrine of the possible, the attainable." We can't run the world, or even our little corner of it, alone. We have to do reconnaissance to find out who will back us up and support us, and who is likely to put up roadblocks. A consultant had to arrange for an appointment with a United States senator to secure his support in obtaining federal clearance for a factory to be constructed in his state. The consultant came armed with voluminous supporting information, but the senator, after hearing his opening remarks, had only one succinct question: Who's for it and who's against it? The answers satisfied him, and he helped push the project through.

The senator's question is a good one to apply in sizing up any important choice/decision project: Who is apt to be for it, and who is apt to be against it?

7. IS THIS A DECISION FOR YOU TO DO SOMETHING, OR MERELY TO RECOMMEND? Theoretically, if you are merely recommending, you should make the same decision you would make if you were responsible for the action (given the same authority as the one to whom you are recommending the action). But are you sure you are working on it in that light? Are you coming to a conclusion that carries more risk than you would assume if you were in the final decision maker's shoes? Have you given sufficient weight to the repercussions on him or her? Are you ready to take your share of any backlash?

How anonymous will you be in regard to the outcome? If you will be anonymous, are you hiding behind that condition regarding touchy aspects of the situation? How about credit for a successful outcome? How much are you allowing your getting or not getting credit to influence you?

How forthright are you willing to be in your final recommendation? Are you tempted to allow yourself, for whatever reason, to recommend something with which you privately disagree? If so, this boils down to the cynical prescription, "Tell them what they want to hear." There may be persuasive reasons to call for this tactic, but any conflict with a deeply held core of beliefs calls for a careful consideration of Proposition 10.

8. DOES THE CHOICE CONFRONTING YOU CONCERN A ONE-TIME SITUATION, OR ONE THAT COULD RECUR? If it is one-time, an important consideration is that there is presumably no danger of setting a precedent. The recommendation can then be considered without concern over possible future entanglements.

If it is a situation that could recur, the matter of precedent assumes importance (cf. Category Five, "Fallout"). How will this affect the policy statement (if one exists) that applies? Have possible hardship cases and other possible needs for exceptions been thought through? (Cf. Category Seven, "Implementation.")

Again, in the case of a recurring situation, how can the correct decision be "programmed" so that similar situations in the future can be handled automatically, without the choice/decision process having to be gone through repeatedly?

9. WHAT ARE THE LONG-RANGE VS. THE SHORT-RANGE CONSEQUENCES THAT WILL PROBABLY RESULT FROM THIS DECISION? One criterion of a person's maturity is the ability and proneness to think of long-term as well as short-term consequences of a projected action. One need hardly belabor the apparently built-in human propensity to disregard the most obvious long-range consequences in favor of immediate gratification: drug addiction, irresponsible sex, drinking before driving— the whole sorry litany.

Examples in the business world are not hard to come by either. Witness problems about toxic wastes, air pollution, exposure of factory workers to harmful and even fatal work environments. In less reprehensible but costly instances, managements have been known to slash research and development expenditures to improve a short-run profit-and-loss statement. The same holds true for advertising: a consumer product can be "milked" for extraordinary immediate profits if advertising is eliminated or cut severely.

10. WILL THE DECISION BE ABSOLUTELY IRREVOCABLE? After "...ten—blast-off!" there's nothing the launchers of a rocket or spaceship can do about calling off the launch, other than triggering some self-destruct circuit. Fortunately, most decisions are not that irrevocable, although the "change-your-mind" option can be extremely narrow and distasteful.

Come to think of it, the absolutely irrevocable decisions you can make are quite limited. (Suicide? Murder? Burning your house down?) So it behooves you not to harbor the notion of irrevocability, and to be sure to consider every feasible option if the decision you make doesn't work out. As a matter of fact, how fast a decision can be reversed or aborted if it is wrong may be as important in sizing up a choice/decision situation as are the monetary and other factors. The celebrated decision-reversal by Coca-Cola Co. to reinstate the old-fashioned Coca-Cola as "Coca-Cola Classic" demonstrated how even the most thoroughly researched corporate decision can come a cropper.

Questions to be asked at change-your-mind time:

a. What would it cost, and how much dislocation would result, if the decision were aborted at certain stages? Have you set up stages one, two, three, etc.? Do you have "Checkpoint Charlie" positions at which you can take readings?

b. Will you be able to establish fall-back strategies for preplanned changes under adverse scenarios?

c. Is worry about personal embarrassment keeping you from reversing a decision when all logic and obvious repercussions demand that needed action?

d. What can you do to put the best possible face upon the situation? Memoranda...public announcements...news releases...explanations to friends and family?

e. Can you backtrack before taking any action? Sometimes you can withdraw from a proposed action before even entering into it, by going back to a previously established position.

11. IS THIS SOMETHING THAT HAS TO REMAIN HUSH-HUSH UNTIL THE VERY LAST MOMENT? If so, what are the reasons for the demand for secrecy? Is there something morally, legally, or ethically shady about the matter? Will pursuing the choice/decision process produce a conflict with your core of beliefs? (Cf. Propositions 10 and 11.)

Who shall be on your "need to know" list? How will the secrecy requirement affect how your necessary research and analysis are to be carried out?

12. SHOULD YOU "BLOW THE WHISTLE" IF YOU DIS-COVER SHENANIGANS BY A HIGHER AUTHORITY? This is a variant of the issue raised in the preceding question. Realistically viewed, if a person's job is on the line, if he has mortgage payments to meet and college tuition bills to pay, hesitation to act with unflinching integrity is quite understandable. Let's consider your options:

a. Miscreants should be exposed, double-dealing should be brought to light, and malfeasance should be punished. But are you obligated to make personal sacrifice, inevitably shared by family members and others dependent upon you, in order to bring down the offenders? You can simply close your eyes, and let someone else do the exposing— no guilt for the wrongdoing would devolve upon you. But wouldn't your silence mean that you are to a degree an accessory? Will there be a gnawing of conscience? Can you live with that?

b. Should you simply quit your job, and say nothing? Pro: You have washed your hands of the matter. Con: Aside from sawing yourself from the payroll, you have the frustration of knowing the perpetrators are continuing in their skullduggery.

c. Should you pilfer incriminating evidence, maybe making copies of revealing documents and passing them along to the media, but exacting a promise of anonymity? A notorious instance was the affair of the *Pentagon Papers*. Daniel Ellsberg, a government employee, furnished the *New York Times* with photocopies of significant portions of a 1969 study commissioned by Secretary of Defense Robert S. McNamara. The study revealed miscalculation, bureaucratic arrogance, and deception on the part of U.S. policymakers, and found that the government had continually resisted full disclosure of increasing military involvement in Southeast Asia long before the American public was informed. Mr. Ellsberg apparently satisfied his conscience as to the propriety of pilfering the information and giving (or selling?) it to the *Times* while still accepting paychecks from his employer, the government. (Ellsberg's anonymity was short-lived. He was indicted for conspiracy, theft, and espionage, but on May 11, 1983, a federal court dismissed all charges.)

No one can tell you which of the above options to choose. It depends upon the nature and strength of your evidence, the nature and strength of your core of beliefs, and your willingness to put your job on the line. It's up to you.

Marshaling the Evidence

W hen there are a lot of data available, you will probably find that the best manager is the one who can ask the right questions. Here are some questions to try on for size:

1. HAVE YOU IDENTIFIED THE SIGNIFICANT VARIABLES IN THE PROBLEM BEFORE YOU? Fortunately there appears to be a law of chance at work, which is referred to by statistical analysts as the Pareto effect, or the maldistribution principle. It can be stated in this way: While most measured results are actually the cumulative effect of many causes, a small minority of the causes account for the major share of the total effect. The large majority of causes is responsible for a very small share of the total effect.

Experience shows that the principle works in every field of endeavor. In selling, 20 percent or less of the accounts will usually be responsible for 80 percent or more of the total volume. In a product line, a few items will account for most of the profits. In manufacturing, when all losses due to substandard products are broken down by product, it is generally found that only a few are responsible for more than half of the losses.

Are you getting the kind of information that will highlight the operative factors?

a. What are the few significant problem areas?

b. For the near term, which areas will show the greatest return for the time, energy, and money expended?

c. For the long term, where will the best payoff be?

d. Are you taking into consideration the personal bias that may influence the judgment of those offering opinions as to what constitutes the problem areas?

2. HAVE YOU STATED THE DECISION OBJECTIVE IN THE MOST SIGNIFICANT WAY? Bringing significant variables to the forefront may well lead to a reconsideration of the way the objective was stated in the first place. This was alluded to in Category Two, "Sizing Up," Question 4, but the point is worth repeating here. You may want to change the whole direction of your thinking.

a. Have you reduced your decision objective to writing? It pays to make this the first step. If you do, you can avoid false starts and keep further efforts on track.

b. Are you guarding against preconception? Professor Erwin H. Schell of MIT, who inspired several generations of students in his classes in engineering and industrial management, used to hammer home the following point:

> The most serious error in administration is the *initial* error. At the beginning of your thinking, you may define your problem incompletely or omit some vital but inconspicuous element. This mistake will obscure your later thinking. Few people are entirely free from prejudices or preconceptions. Almost everyone has a mental blind spot that causes him to underestimate or overlook something important. *The greatest curse of thought is preconception.*

3. ARE YOU SUBCONSCIOUSLY SCREENING OUT UNFAVORABLE EVIDENCE? This is quite a common failing, a child of wishful thinking, and is related to the point about preconceptions just made. It takes the form of closing the eyes and ears and mind to evidence not conducive to or in actual opposition to a desired outcome.

4. ARE YOU ALERT TO THE "RESPONSE BIAS" IN YOUR PERSONAL IN-DEPTH INTERVIEWING? Where teams of interviewers are sent into the field with questionnaires, this personality factor is difficult, if not impossible, to allow for. However, the point should be kept in mind if you are basing a decision in whole or in part on a few highly selective, probing conversations with a small number of knowledgeable persons with whose backgrounds and general behavior patterns you are familiar.

It need hardly be added that one must also be on guard against opinions and information from well-wishers and apple-polishers. It is always beguiling to hear the kind of news you want to hear—but pinch yourself and ask whether some discounting is called for.

5. IS THE UPWARD FLOW OF VITAL INFORMATION PROPERLY STRUCTURED INTO THE DECISION-MAKING PROCESS? In a large organization, it is obvious that several layers of management must intervene between top decision making and ultimate implementation at the "front line" operating level. Without such a hierarchy of command no large organization could achieve its purposes. However, the fact remains that in very large (and even not so large) organizations, the gap between the seat of decisions and the scene of actions is so great that decisions of the most far-reaching consequences are made in a mental environment totally removed from the hardships and dust and turmoil of the world where they must be carried out. ("Let them eat cake," said Marie Antoinette when informed that the masses had no bread to eat.)

6. ARE YOU EFFECTIVELY ORGANIZED TO SECURE THE NEEDED DATA? Questions to check should include:

a. What kind of data are required? External? Internal? How should the activities to gather the data be prioritized?

b. What data should be available from current internal reporting? What minimal changes in existing routines are possible to furnish the information needed? What arrangements can be made with heads of departments to compile the needed data?

c. For external data—industry, economics, sociopolitical, technological—what is available from ongoing sources such as literature searches, governmental agencies, and trade associations? For trend data, how far back would it be reasonable to go?

d. What data gathering should be contracted for? Have you clearly stated the requirements in writing? What are the budgetary limitations for such research? How can the competence of the survey organization under consideration be ascertained? What explicit quality controls can be established? Have you assured confidentiality of the findings? Have you set penalties for nonperformance? Have you scheduled interim reports of progress?

e. Should any data-gathering procedures set up be made a continuing routine for ongoing decisional purposes?

f. What facilities are available for computer processing of quantitative data?

g. What arrangements should be made for preparation, printing, and distribution of the final report?

7. ARE YOU AVAILING YOURSELF OF THE OPINIONS AND SUGGESTIONS OF YOUR OWN PERSONNEL? This comes under the head of "finding diamonds in your own backyard." With respect to decisions having to do with employee-relations policies and with internal procedures, managements are prone to pay large per diems to consultants for surveys of operations, without having taken the trouble themselves to consult supervisors and key employees. Supervisors and key employees may be fully aware of wastes and inefficiencies, but may never have never been given the opportunity to express themselves.

8. FOR BUSINESS DECISIONS HAVING TO DO WITH PROD-
UCTS AND MARKETING, HAVE YOU MADE A SYSTEM-
ATIC EFFORT TO SECURE OPINIONS AND SUGGESTIONS
FROM KEY CUSTOMERS?   This is another version of "diamonds in your own backyard." For consumer products,
companies use questionnaires sent to purchasers at a fixed
time after receipt of a self-addressed warranty card. In industrial marketing, where users are relatively few as com-
pared with mass marketing and where there is more direct,
personal relationship with key customers, in-depth information can be obtained by personal contact.

9. ARE YOU MAKING FULL USE OF ONE-TO-ONE PER-
SONAL CONTACTS? Obviously, in researching for any
significant decision, you will have to rely heavily on
secondhand information—survey results conducted by
outsiders, in-house gleanings from pertinent literature,
and reports by subordinates. But to get the "feel" of the
situation, personal one-to-one contacts with information sources must be added to the input.
   Experience shows that in business, people are generally disposed to be friendly and informative in discussing
experiences and sharing opinions—witness the sharing
done at conferences of the American Management Association, the Conference Board, and other business research organizations. The attitude is usually the
professional one of sharing, provided there is no prying
into classified matters.

10. IF YOU ARE A TOP EXECUTIVE, HAVE YOU SET UP
BARRIERS AGAINST BAD NEWS? In earlier times, the
king was wont to behead the bearer of bad news. In
modern times this impulse lingers on in the corporate
suite, not in such a sanguinary form, but effectively,
nevertheless. It leads to the exodus of good men and
women to a more favorable environment, or to their

transformation into yes-men and yes-women. The organization can't win.

11. ARE YOUR INPUTS REASONABLY COMPLETE? Remember the point about analysis paralysis. When should you "close the books" on information gathering, and begin the process of weighing the evidence and finalizing the choice/decision process?

It is not possible to give a universal Rx. The only sure answer is, "It all depends." That may be unsatisfactory, but some observations will be helpful:

a. What possible events or circumstances would be of overriding importance in dictating change, postponement, or shutdown of a project under way or under consideration? List the contingencies for which your receptors must always be open: enemy attack, public or employee safety and health, indications of adverse public-relations fallout. Can you judge the probability of such eventualities occurring, and their effect upon the project you have in mind?

b. Is a striving for unneeded perfection holding up the conclusion of information gathering? For business decisions, information gathering is of course not limited to customer and public surveys. The choice/decision may rest upon information gleaned in laboratory tests, or in checking and double-checking computations, or in searching out case examples to bolster a recommendation. An overdeveloped sense of perfection may lead to your doing or authorizing this sort of work over and over again, continually holding up final decision and action for more and more information.

When to stop will have to be a subjective determination. The seasoned decision maker keeps the gathering of ever more quantitative information in perspective. The weight of information already received may be such that a few more statistics would not change the picture. While the determination is subjective, that is not to say that it is arbitrary or capricious. The "feel" for readiness to act is based on reason, experience, and common sense.

c. How much of your raw findings can be preliminarily formulated, on the premise that the final result would not change much in any event?

Weighing the Evidence

How shall you go about weighing pros and cons? Here are important considerations:

1. ARE YOU CONSIDERING THE SOURCE? Don't ask a barber whether you need a haircut. Are information, advice, or suggestions tainted with self-interest? Misleading inputs are, of course, not always intentional. The wrong kind of people may have been contacted, or the wrong kinds of questions asked. As indicated in the preceding Category, bias and prejudice must be taken into account, and as discussed later herein, the opinions of experts must be judged in the light of their specialties—"where they're coming from." Finally, you must steel yourself to be ruthlessly objective where welcome opinions and advice are given. Subservience, fear, politeness, respect, and awe of a questioner's position and reputation are well-known inhibitors of candor—as, for reasons of selective blindness, are respect, love, and affection.

2. ARE YOU JUMPING TO A CONCLUSION? Epictetus sounded a caveat some two thousand years ago: "Be not swept off your feet by the vividness of the impression, but say, 'Impression, wait for me a little. Let me see what you are and what you represent. Let me try you.'"

When at first blush things look especially good, it's always well to pinch yourself. Things are not always what they seem. It may be well to point out here that statistical correlations may upon closer examination turn out not to be indicative of a true relationship, and must always be put to the test of common sense. For example, in summer consumption of ice cream in the United States jumps to an astronomical high. Unfortunately, deaths by drowning reach seasonal highs at the same time. If you match the two curves, will you conclude that consumption of ice cream causes drowning?

3. WHAT IS THE CREDIBILITY CATEGORY OF THE EVIDENCE? Is it (a) scientific—i.e., quantitatively measurable and replicable? Or (b) anecdotal? Or (c) subjective—mere expression of opinion? What verification is possible and called for?

4. TO WHAT EXTENT ARE YOU ABLE TO QUANTIFY RISKS? WHAT ARE THE ODDS? Most mathematical formulas for assessing risks and developing strategies have probability factors built into them. These are often quite subjective, sometimes labeled "best estimate," with alternatives of "optimistic," "pessimistic," or "best scenario," "worst scenario." Their subjectivity is often lost

sight of by a decision maker confronted with choices set forth by analysts in neat quantitative terms.

Few probability computations permit the highly accurate assessments one can make in the illustrations cited in statistical textbooks when they speak of the chances of heads or tails or heads-tails sequences in the toss of a coin, or the numerical chance of throwing a seven with two dice, or of drawing an inside straight in poker. In real life, the coins are not perfectly balanced, the dice may be loaded, the dealer may have marked the cards. Only when the influences of chance or chicanery have been eliminated or with confidence reduced to insignificance can the computed probabilities be effectively relied upon.

Here a word is in order about the distinction between uncertainty and risk. Clear definitions are offered by Donald A. Schon:

> *Risk* has its place in a calculus of probabilities. It lends itself to quantitative expression—as when we say that the chances of finding a defective part out of 100 in a batch are two. In the framework of benefit-cost analysis, the risk of an innovation is how much we stand to lose if we fail, multiplied by the probability of that failure....*Uncertainty* is quite another matter: A situation is uncertain when it requires action but resists analysis of risks. For example, a gambler takes a risk in an honest game of blackjack when, knowing the odds, he calls for another card. But the same gambler, unsure of the honesty of the game, is in a situation of uncertainty.— "The Fear of Innovation," *International Science and Technology*, Nov. 1966.

Clearly, it is good to have as much hard, quantifiable data as possible, and to glean whatever you can from statistical analysis and mathematical manipulations. However, there are some pitfalls to watch out for:

a. Are you properly looking behind quantitative findings? In even the most precise-looking quantitative analyses you have to look behind the figures to keep from being misled. Computer simulation is a case in point. The real world is so complex, so prone to impingement by unpredictable and/or unmeasurable influences, and so continually changing, that even the most elaborate of mathematical models are only approximations of the dust and turmoil and dynamism of the real world. They are no more "real" than a good road map (even an updated one) is in relation to the trees and rocks and streams of the landscape through which it seeks to guide you.

b. Are you lulled into a false sense of security by a "high probability" assessment? You may be justified in giving high credence to the opinion of analysts as to the probability of certain results, assuming certain prior conditions, and you may feel comfortable with an 85 percent assessment. But if a chain of events is involved, each one also having a probability of success of 85 percent, the relatively high rating will quickly erode if your project calls for the successful outcome of all. The successful outcome for two events would be only 72 percent probable, and of three only 61 percent. And if a fourth is involved, the overall success rating would fall to 52 percent.

c. How good are the numbers? Impressive projections based on government or trade association statistics, or survey or opinion-poll results, are no better than the underlying figures. A good policy is to look at all of those with a jaundiced eye. Government figures notoriously suffer from a long time-lag between the date of reporting and today's date. Economic indicators are useful tools only when used with an awareness of their imperfections:

> The leading indicators sometimes foreshadow downturns by a year or more, sometimes only a few months. They sometimes emit false signals, suggesting recession when all that occurs is a slowdown.... And government figures on specific industries are no better than the reports and estimates submitted by companies in the field, and care is exercised to prevent disclosures that would identify specific companies or otherwise reveal proprietary information. Trade association figures and figures compiled by trade publications are more up-to-date than government figures, but often contain an undisclosed amount of estimates and guestimates.—Geoffrey H. Moore, "Those Misleading Economic Indicators," The *New York Times*, March 16, 1986.

d. What is your ingrained attitude toward risk? Two people may look at the same assessment of risk and come up with totally different choices/decisions. The reason is that they are not two identically programmed robots viewing identical computer printouts. Your choice depends upon whether you're constitutionally disposed to take relatively larger risks for the possibility of significantly larger gains, or would rather play it safe by choosing a practically sure but relatively modest gain. You probably cannot do much to change an ingrained propensity to gamble or not to gamble— but you can make yourself constantly aware of it, and so be able to choose more objectively in any given situation.

If your organization's culture is one of relatively high accommodation of risk for high returns, you will be well advised to check any contemplated recommendation or action against a propensity you may have toward overcaution. And by the same token, in a conservative organization your vigilance should be turned in the opposite direction.

5. HOW ARE YOU HANDLING DECISION-MAKING FACTORS THAT DEFY QUANTIFICATION? Although this area has been designated in the Schon distinction cited above as one of "uncertainty," it is by no means true that it cannot be evaluated.

Discussions elsewhere in this book offer pointers to help weigh evidence that is not quantifiable, but let us here say a few words about intuition. That is the faculty brought into play whenever choice/decisions must be made and action taken in the absence of explicit persuasive indicators. Here is Webster's definition:

> **intuition:** Knowledge obtained, or the power of knowing, without recourse to inference or reasoning; innate or instinctive knowledge; insight; familiarity, a quick or ready insight or apprehension.

That is the everyday concept of the word, and is the way it is used here. But the position taken here is that contrary to popular belief, intuition is by no means to be considered some inexplicable extra-sensory gift that produces sound choices with no discernible logical foundation. In this view, one would not trust the "intuition" of a child, but would listen respectfully to an experienced, "seasoned" person's assessment of evidence, and the probable outcomes of suggested alternatives—in the area of his or her applicable expertise. By the same token one would discount the much vaunted "women's intuition" unless, similarly, it were based on expertise and experience.

Let us distinguish between two ways in which intuition is commonly discussed. The first has to do with precognition—as when someone says, "I *knew* something bad was going to happen to Aunt Tilda, and sure enough, her house was broken into last week and her silver serving set was stolen." If you look further into this incident, you'll probably find that (a) there has been a spate of burglaries on Aunt Tilda's block, indicating a good likelihood that sooner or later her house would be on the list; and (b) the person recounting the premonition was a born "worrier," prone to conjuring up all kinds of dire happenings, and keeping no record on hits and misses. We need spend no more time on such stories beyond restating the position taken here: Analysis will always provide normal, common-sense explanations for the alleged "intuitions."

It is the second way in which intuition is commonly discussed that is of interest in our present context. This refers to the apparent innate capacity, without apparent recourse to inference or deduction, which some people bring to choice/decision with a high degree of success—where there are no clear-cut quantitative assessments of evidence or reliable probability estimates.

Admittedly, a high degree of foresight seems to be involved, but this is not precognition in the form of an extrasensory faculty as discussed by researchers in parapsychology. Rather, for the "seasoned operator," the intuition is a short-cut process of quickly cutting through nonessentials, spotting pitfalls not readily apparent to others because they were not looked for…sensing possible resistance to change…being alert to human factors of pride, fear, jealousy, and just plain dunderheadedness; …and knowing what can work and what won't work…and what surprises may lurk down the road.

a. To what extent are you relying upon your intuition, in the above sense of innate capacity, without recourse to inference or deductive reasoning? Are you really in the class of the seasoned operator described above? Perhaps for most of us the safe procedure must still be to think very carefully before heeding too readily the voice of what we presume to be intuition. Wishful thinking and expediency often assume her guise. If you are of an age at which most of your experience still lies ahead of you, tread warily!

Take comfort in the point stressed here, that intuition isn't something that you are "born" with, that you either have or don't have. Intuition in our second sense is an acquired skill. Your genes may determine the speed with which you can acquire it if you put your mind to it. But few people use more than a fraction of their capacity to excel in the direction that their genes bestow upon them; thus the lesser endowed can in the long run surpass their more fortunate rivals.

b. To what extent can you rely on the intuition of others? Certain caveats must be kept in mind:

(1) Is the decision before you one calling for imagination and innovation? If so, will a recommendation based upon the intuition of a veteran executive or key person, or mentor in a personal matter, perhaps suffer from overconcern with traditional ways of doing things?

(2) Where technology is concerned, has he or she kept up to date on technological developments?

(3) Is there a chance that the "intuition" relied upon is marred by the NIH ("Not-Invented-Here") syndrome?

(4) Are the conditions surrounding the pro-

jected decision so different from those in which operations have previously been conducted that the value of intuition based on prior experience is severely eroded?

If we seem to have devoted an inordinate amount of space to intuition, it is because it plays so important and necessary a role in the choice/decision process. This role is too greatly denigrated by the "management scientists" in their dedication to mathematical techniques. At the same time, it must be recognized that probably the greatest contributor to poor decisions is reliance upon something that is deemed to be dependable intuition but is not. Unless you heed caveats mentioned herein, you will run the risk of being victimized by wishful thinking or unsupported hunch, or of being lulled by welcome but false evaluation of an advisor whose intuition is *pseudo* because there is no match of background to present circumstance.

6. HOW AN YOU JUDGE THE OPINIONS OF EXPERTS? In this day and age (and it was probably true in any age) we are all at the mercy of experts. It is simply not possible to follow Descartes's first precept in his "Discourse on Method," namely:

> ...never to accept anything as true which I did not know to be manifestly so, that is, carefully to avoid precipitancy and bias, and to include nothing in my judgments except what presented itself so clearly and distinctly to my mind that I would never have occasion to doubt it.

If you are a final decision maker, there are no two ways about it—you have to rely on experts.

If you are well grounded in the professional/technical aspects of the problem calling for choice and decision, you are in a good position to move confidently in the face of conflicting advice, even if it involves second-guessing the experts. The acute problem arises when a generalist must decide matters that go beyond his personal expertise. It is on your track record of such judgments that an evaluation of your business and personal leadership will rest. The degree of confidence you can place upon the inputs of experts calls for considerations such as the following:

a. What is the central thrust of their expertise? How does this align with the specialization called for by the problem at hand? The chief executive of a large computer manufacturing company put it this way (his own background was legal, not scientific or engineering):

> I don't put too much weight on the opinion of the head of our research as to whether the design innovation he is so excited about will sell. And I don't base our five-year budget projections exclusively on the inputs from my chief economist or head of sales. The economist tells me what the economic weather is likely to be, but *I* decide whether to plan for a picnic in the sun or to wear overshoes and carry an umbrella. And I temper the exuberance of the sales head with whatever grains of salt are necessary.

b. Where are the experts "coming from"? What do their previous actions and pronouncements tell about their value-judgment base beyond the horizons of their specialties? How do these relate to the moral and ethical, as well as the material, aspects of the undertaking?

c. What about the fallout implicit in the experts' recommendations? Specialists frequently do not anticipate the wider repercussions of their activities (and sometimes, perhaps, are not especially interested in them), e.g., air pollution and toxic wastes. In his book *The Knowledge Executive*, Harlan Cleveland noted:

> It is still shocking, 40 years later, to realize that the Manhattan Project, the huge secret organization that produced the atom bomb during World War II, did not employ on its staff a single person whose full-time assignment was to think hard about the policy implications of the project should it succeed. Thus no one was working on nuclear arms control. We have been playing catch-up, not too successfully, ever since.

7. CAVEATS. Here are some caveats for the decision maker who is evaluating the advice of experts:

a. When considering recommendations from a group, remember that the decision of each member of a group may very well have been influenced by his or her expectation of the behavior of other members of the group. And perhaps the recommendation of the group was merely a rubber-stamping of the choice/decision of a dynamic leader.

b. Don't let your perception of evidence be colored by wishful thinking. Are you looking at something through rose-colored glasses? Or through green-colored ones (the grass often looks greener on the other side of the fence)?

c. Don't be misled by the halo effect. This is a term used by psychologists in connection with performance appraisal, referring to a common tendency to overvalue a person's ability in one line of effort because of his or her outstanding performance in something else. In our present context this applies to giving greater than warranted weight to opinions expressed on a given issue because of the enunciator's eminence in an unrelated field.

d. When you are presented with nonconfirming evidence, be aware of the difference between accepting something as a dismissable exception to a general rule or as a warning flag to reconsider a strong tentative conclusion.

e. Discount for politeness. People may be telling you what they think you want to hear, or what they think will avoid offending or embarrassing you.

f. Make allowances for the aging and adequacy of evidence. Information that was applicable a number of years ago may not be relevant to a similar situation today. And opinions or recounted experiences of a few vocal sources may not be representative of your area of interest.

g. Question your assumptions. Probe for hidden, unsuspected assumptions possibly underlying significant aspects of the problem at hand.

CATEGORY FIVE

Fallout

There may be repercussions that were impossible (practically speaking) to foresee at the time of choice/decision, as in the long, dragged out case of the Johns-Manville victims of exposure to asbestos, where results were long delayed. Or totally unexpected and disconcerting results may be immediate, as in the case of the quick public clamor after Coca-Cola's$^{®}$ launching of its famous "New Coke." Others may have been recognized but not guarded against, either because of overconfidence ("It can't happen here"), or because of a willingness to take unjustifiable risks. Let us take up the questions that must be considered in order to face probable fallout *before* the final choice/decision is made:

1. WHAT PERSONAL OR FAMILY SACRIFICES ARE YOU CONTEMPLATING? Is the game worth the candle? An executive confided that one of the decisions he regretted most, made earlier in his career when he was still struggling to get to the top, was to miss his elder daughter's high-school graduation because he felt he had to cancel a flight home in order to stay and solve a client's problem. "Imagine doing that for a *business* reason!" he said. He swore that barring physical restraint, he would never again miss one of his children's "rites of passage." And he kept that promise. "You almost always have a chance to recoup a monetary loss," he said, "but how can you recoup a missed graduation?"

2. ARE YOU SACRIFICING LONG-TERM GAINS FOR SHORT-TERM BENEFITS? Observers of the business scene have noted a tendency of corporate managements in recent years to emphasize short-run financial results— this year's bottom line, price/earnings ratios, wheeler-dealer takeovers—rather than showing a dedication to a product or service and a desire to build for the future instead of striving for stock-market performance. Lawrence Miller, in his book *American Spirit*, expresses this attitude succinctly:

> During recent decades there has arisen a cadre of executives at the top of our corporations who have served more to destroy purpose than to create it. These anti-leaders have put together some of the largest conglomerates in the nation. They have done so not by building a business, but by the organization of finances. Many of them have never made an item, delivered a service, or sold a product to an actual customer...the managers who must run the businesses understand that they are judged now only on financial criteria, not on the merits of advancing the state of technology, producing the highest-quality product, or being respected by customers.

3. WILL THERE BE (FOR GOOD AND SUFFICIENT REA-
SONS) AN APPRECIABLE TIME LAG BEFORE THIS DECISION
IS MADE KNOWN TO THOSE IT AFFECTS? If so, be prepared for the rumor mill to begin grinding away. Should
reasons for the delayed promulgation be reconsidered? If
they cannot, what can be done to counteract false information?

Can rumor mills be controlled? Not very easily,
because once a story gets buzzing around, people's
minds work like individual newspapers. They remember
and pass along the original story in headline type, and
treat attempts to straighten out distortions in small print
on page eighteen.

One trouble is that there is usually just enough truth
in the story going the rounds to make it sound credible.
Review your communications procedures. Brief key people on exactly what can be said in response to queries.
If the decision presages bad news—plant closings, layoffs, a hostile merger, etc.—be as reassuring as you can,
but don't sugarcoat.

4. WHO SHOULD BE INFORMED OF DECISIONS? The
point here is not about employee-relations announcements as discussed above, but rather about information for participants in the decision-making process,
and for others immediately concerned with implementation.

Communication is discussed under Category Seven,
"Implementation." However, failure to tell all concerned
can be a significant cause of detrimental fallout. The late
celebrated radio personality Fred Allen made famous the
phrase, "*Why doesn't anyone TELL me these things?*"
Don't jeopardize effectiveness by justifying the Allen
complaint.

Where a decision or recommendation comes out of
conference or committee deliberations, it will be well to

review the following list on the preparation and distribution of minutes:

a. Minutes should be carefully edited for ambiguous or otherwise unclear terminology. This is especially important if some of the participants were not particularly versed in the technical jargon involved.

b. Send a copy of the minutes to all participants. There can be exceptions for nongroup participants who may have been brought in—perhaps for a brief period—for expertise pertinent to the decision. It may not be advisable to distribute minutes to them. But if the experts' contribution was extensive, at least a memorandum should be sent for their review, giving the gist of their remarks, as a matter of courtesy and of insuring accuracy.

c. Should minutes go to others? It may well be that certain interested persons who were not at the meeting should get minutes, for their information.

d. Should there be individual follow-up discussion of the minutes? If the meeting discussion has been intricate, highly technical, or highly controversial, consider discussing the minutes with certain participants to be sure that they have a clear understanding of what was decided.

e. Should subsequent, related information be included? Where logic demands, the minutes need not be confined entirely to discussion held at the conference itself. A related point, checked after the meeting for clarification, may be included. An exception will be a conference where a strictly verbatim transcript is required for legal purposes.

However, where additional information is included, the minutes should clearly designate it as such.

5. HOW WILL THE DECISION SIT WITH CONFLICTING AIMS OF PERSONS OR GROUPS AFFECTED? Run through the possibilities ahead of time, to be properly prepared for flak. You are not running a popularity contest, and must expect some resistance and resentments under the best of conditions—but it will pay to identify all possible opposition. This will not only help shape the decision, but will also smooth the path of implementation. In business situations, keep in mind the conflicting aims of sales, credit, production, and finance, to say nothing of customer interests and goodwill. Keep your sensing antennae extended. What is the best way to present the situation? How can ruffled feathers be smoothed?

6. WHAT OTHER PREVIOUSLY MADE AND PROMULGATED DECISION(S) WILL HAVE TO BE CHANGED OR RESCINDED? Take stock of this *before* promulgating the new decision: conflicting instructions and guidelines can engender serious fallout. If policy and procedure manuals are in use, be sure that inoperative statements are altered or removed.

If the changed signals imply that you were wrong about the superseded decision, so be it. Don't waste time fretting about "losing face." Simply state the positive reasons for the change, and let it go at that.

7. ARE YOU CLOSING YOUR EYES TO THE DANGER OF SOME EVENTUALITY SIMPLY BECAUSE OF ITS REMOTENESS? Cigarette smoking is a prime example of this failing. Reams could be written about the insanity of allowing cigarette advertising in the print media while

banning it on the air—but the really inexplicable part of this state of affairs is the fact that despite the barrage of admonitions and mandates and clearly visible warnings by the Surgeon General appearing on the slick magazine ads, people (including many medical doctors) imperturbably continue to smoke and even chain-smoke. This is undoubtedly a combination of the "It can't happen to me" syndrome and Scarlett O'Hara's "I'll worry about that tomorrow."

The closing-of-eyes phenomenon can also affect business decisions. For example, many a top-level executive simply refuses to face his inevitable retirement. Logic makes him perceive the significance of the calendar, but his mind won't react to the facts. He mesmerizes himself into thinking that the date remains remote, and takes no steps to groom a successor. Quite the contrary—no second-in-command ever satisfies him; he finds fault with every one of them. Higher management may force his hand, but if it doesn't, the calendar will make its inevitable advance, and the result will be disorganization and disruption.

8. REMEMBER THE "BALANCE OF NATURE." In his book *Administrative Behavior*, Herbert A. Simon warns public officials against the danger of assuming that a state of "all other things being equal" prevails. He points out that one outcome that is good may produce a change that makes some other output bad. Cutting the cost of operating a purchasing activity may result in uneconomic purchasing...cutting public payrolls may increase the welfare load...paying Peter may rob Paul, perhaps unwittingly. In the business milieu, companies have decided to expand market share by direct selling to certain classes of accounts, only to find that relations with their network of jobbers and dealers have been strained.

Note that nothing in the foregoing should be construed as an argument against innovation. The admonition here is to be aware of the "balance of nature," to think about possible fallouts and to take them into account.

9. TO WHAT EXTENT SHOULD HUMANE CONSIDERATIONS AFFECT THE DECISION? Some decisions—e.g., those referring to plant closings, layoffs and discharge, budget crunches, and the like—will inevitably mean that some people will be adversely affected. Nevertheless, responsible executive action must follow. Here are some questions that should be brought to bear:

a. Should humane considerations dictate that a less than economically optimum decision be adopted?

b. Will there be hardship cases? Will it be possible to make special allowances for them?

c. Should postponement of the originally contemplated decision be made, for easier adjustment by those adversely affected?

d. Should, on second thought, the proposed decision be entirely scratched?

10. WILL THE DECISION SET A PRECEDENT? Prudence dictates that you look ahead to all possible contingencies. An example in point: A research director thought he was establishing sound policy when, for his newly created large-scale fundamental research unit, he demanded advanced technical degrees for all research positions, junior as well as senior, and for many positions which were essentially at the technician level. Under this system, there was no place for most of the young professional men and women to go consistent with their ambitions and training. By the time this became apparent, many of them had lost valuable years. The director's personnel problems mounted, and he complained that he was spending more time arranging transfers and finding replacements than furthering his research mission. He had set a precedent without looking into the consequences.

11. WHAT ARE THE PUBLIC RELATIONS IMPLICATIONS? Today, more than ever before, corporations are operating in what has been termed a "pressure cooker" environment. They are under siege from consumer advocates, environmentalists, women's lib advocates, civil-righters, and other activist groups. Managements are criticized for investing in companies doing business in South Africa and for establishing their own operations there...for producing armaments or substances used in war...for polluting the atmosphere or poisoning the landscape...and the litany goes on and on. It used to be that a business was castigated for being Big. Now it's castigated for being Big and Bad.

A corporation today is judged not only by a financial audit, but also by a *social audit*; not only by what it does not do in terms of infracting laws, but also by what it goes out of its way to do affirmatively to employ and promote members of minority groups. We have come a long way from Mr. Vanderbilt's "The public be damned."

Check whether the following considerations are pertinent, and if so, whether they are covered:

a. Pollution and wastes: Government standards.

b. OSHA standards.

c. Equal employment opportunity regulations.

d. If ethnic groups are involved, promulgation in appropriate languages.

e. Foreign operations: Avoidance of breaches of religious or societal taboos.

f. Investment decisions: A defined position on activist clamor (e.g., South Africa).

g. Ethics: Conformance with corporate guidelines.

h. Effect on local communities of centrally established policies.

i. Availability of means for promulgating the decision.

12. HOW DO CHANCES OF SUCCESS COMPARE WITH CHANCES OF FAILURE?

a. Is this an issue that must be settled at this time? Would postponement provide time for avoiding or mending broken fences?

b. Would the decision involve a personal confrontation with one of your peers or subordinates? How crucial would it probably be considered by him or her? Will that person's cooperation be needed on a future matter? How does the importance of that future matter compare with the one at hand?

13. WHO WILL GET THE CREDIT FOR A SUCCESSFUL OUTCOME?

a. Who else is involved in the implementation of this decision? Will they shoulder you out of the picture when kudos are passed around? What can you do to forestall that?

b. If things go wrong, how serious a mark (blot?) will that be on your record?

14. WHAT WILL BE THE ATTITUDE OF THE TROOPS IF THE SITUATION BECOMES STICKY? How sure are you of loyalties? How sure are you of backup? Are you new at heading up your unit? Were your key people there ahead of you? If so, can you say that they have fully accepted you? If not, what could be the possible fallout? Would that justify delaying the decision, assuming the decision can be delayed?

a. Is there a key person in your unit with whom you have a special rapport? If so, can he or she be used to dampen any possible adverse fallout?

b. Have you supplanted or been selected over a popular member of your group? Is there lingering resentment and jealousy?

c. Can you expect adverse fallout because your projected decision flies in the face of opposing recommendations or expressed misgivings of specialists or technicians reporting to you? What special steps should you take to inform them of the reasons for your decision (perhaps requirements of the "big picture" of which they may be unaware)?

CATEGORY SIX

Under the Gun

THE FINAL ACT OF DECISION

So the time has come—the moment of truth. But if you've read what's between page 1 and this page, you're not caught unawares. You do not have to take a blind and desperate stab. After you have made the decision, you can be in the enviable position of Winston Churchill, who said that he was always able to sleep soundly after the day's work because he knew that the decisions he had made were the best possible he could have made under the circumstances, and that nothing would be gained by regrets.

What can you do to assure yourself of Mr. Churchill's postdecisional sanguinity? Try the following:

1. CHECK AND DOUBLE-CHECK. For starters, review the applicable precautions we have already discussed, before making the final-final, this-is-it decision. Thus:

a. Are you making the decision under optimum mental and physical conditions?

b. Is your conscience clear? ("Basic Propositions," Questions 10 and 11.)

c. Does your decision rest on a proper balance between short- and long-term considerations? (*Category Two*, Question 9, and *Category Five*, Question 3.)

d. Are you fairly sure of backup—from the troops and from higher echelons? (*Category Five*, Question 14.)

e. Will the decision set a precedent? (*Category Five*, Question 11.)

f. Have you double-checked the "politics" of the situation? What about the personalities involved? (*Category Two*, Question 6.)

g. Are you reasonably sure of implementation? (This point will be elaborated upon in the following chapter, but cf. also "Basic Propositions," Questions 14 and 15.)

h. Will you be able to set up early warning signals to flash if things begin to go wrong? (To be noted here, but this will be discussed in the following chapter.)

i. Will this decision be irrevocable? (*Category Two*, Question 10.)

j. Are you too intent upon defending an earlier position? (*Category One*, Question 2, and *Category Five*, Question 7.)

k. Are you putting intuition under proper scrutiny? (*Category Four*, Question 5.)

2. ARE YOU SURE YOU'RE NOT IN A WHOLE NEW BALL GAME? The failure to recognize that you're in a whole new ball game can be disastrous. The problem arises from erroneously assuming that changes you experienced or foresaw in the milieu are merely changes in *degree*, calling for doing what was done before, only better, when in reality they are changes in *kind*, calling for a whole new way of thinking and acting.

Here you run into one of the most difficult hurdles to overcome in decision making: to shake off the ingrained mental set brought on by earlier successful methods that worked in an earlier operational environment. Your mind refuses even to entertain the idea of a "new world" to which the old tried-and-true concepts and methods are not attuned. Examples in business abound:

> Henry Ford put America on wheels with a dependable, low-priced vehicle. But sticking to the Model T "in any color as long as it's *black*" and a cumbersome gear-shifing mechanism no longer satisfied potential buyers after relative affluence had seeped down to mass markets. These buyers had access to a wide choice of types of cars and degrees of luxury offered by competitors. The old reliable Ford was on a dead-end street when Henry Ford II came on the scene and took the bold new steps needed to revive the company.

> Mass-circulated magazines were American institutions, offering a lively and diversified fare of fiction and nonfiction every week for as little as a nickel to millions of

readers. Then came radio and later television, and the broad-appeal editorial formula no longer worked. *The Saturday Evening Post, Colliers, Life,* and *Liberty* gave up their respective ghosts, while specialized publications appealing to narrowly defined interests flourished.

Wang Laboratories, Inc., which once dominated the office world with word processors, had to file for bankruptcy, having lost its way as the applications of personal computers dramatically broadened in the workplace. At its peak in 1988, Wang employed 31,300 workers. At the time of the filing, employment was down to 13,000, and 5,000 additional employees were set to be released....The market had shifted away from minicomputers, which were a Wang mainstay, to work stations and networks linking personal computers, the very segment in which Wang lagged...and IBM's difficulties and mass layoffs had almost the same root causes.

3. DID YOU MAKE A PILOT RUN? IF NOT, CAN YOU AND SHOULD YOU DO SO, AND IS THERE STILL TIME? Everything may point to having confidence that your projected decision is sound. But for many types of decisions it will always be best to test the water before taking the final plunge.

4. DON'T FALL INTO THE "LET'S GET-IT-OVER-WITH" TRAP. It's up to you to balance two adjurations: "Take all the time the issue deserves, but not a minute more," and "Take all the time you can spare, but not a minute more." Don't decide upon a course of action simply to relieve emotional tension.

5. HAVE YOU USED THE "DEVIL'S ADVOCATE" TECHNIQUE? In training workshops this is called "role reversal." The act of assuming with all possible empathy the motivation of those opposing your position will often provide new insights that will lead to strengthening your own approach. Seeing and *feeling* the other fellow's point of view may even, surprisingly, change your own.

6. IF PUSH COMES TO SHOVE, WHAT ARE THE LIMITS OF CONCESSIONS YOU WILL MAKE? You will have to draw the line somewhere. Better think it through now. What are the acceptable trade-offs?

7. SHOULD YOU SETTLE FOR "SATISFICING"? Herbert A. Simon has given currency to a new meaning for the old Scottish word *satisficing*. He uses it in a decision-making technique that opts for a decision leading to a result which is merely better than an extant situation or condition, as distinguished from maximizing, i.e., arriving at an optimum solution. This is latching on to a decision or solution as soon as one is found that meets certain minimal desiderata rather than exhaustively analyzing and weighing *all* alternatives to arrive at the "ideally best possible" decision.

8. DON'T FORGET THE LINK TO THE FUTURE. Every choice/decision is linked to the future, and the immediate link has a link behind it, and so on. Be especially on guard when you are disposed to make a choice fully knowing that what you are doing cannot stand the light of public exposure on ethical or letter-of-the-law grounds. Take time out to be sure that you not only want what you want, but also that you want what it leads to.

9. ARE YOU WATCHING THE BUCKS? In *Category Five*, Question 3, the discussion inveighed against a tendency in corporate decision making to emphasize short-term financial results rather than to build for the future. Nothing said there is to be construed as requiring a retraction under the present question. However, when you get to decisions made at operating levels, decisions and recommendations sent to higher levels for consideration must be made within commonsense budgetary restraints.

10. IF YOU ARE DISPOSED TO BLUFF, DON'T UNDERESTIMATE THE INTELLIGENCE, ACUMEN, AND STAYING POWER OF YOUR OPPONENTS OR COMPETITORS. It could be fatal.

Implementation

> Glendower: *I can call the spirits from the vastly deep!*
> Hotspur: *Why, so can I, or so can any man; but will they come when you do call for them?*
>
> *Shakespeare,* King Henry IV

An unenforceable or logically unworkable decision is not a decision. A decision that does not result in action, even though it may be theoretically workable, is not a decision. The old mouse, in Aesop's fable of the mice who voted to pin a bell on the cat's tail, reminds us that "it's easy to propose impossible remedies." Let's see what is involved:

1. **HAVE YOU SPIKED THE HOSTILE GUNS?** Your prior explorations will probably have indicated certain quarters where acquiescence was given grudgingly and perhaps after open opposition. Now that the die is cast, it

will behoove you to go out of your way to conciliate and persuade the foot draggers.

You can take a leaf from the politician's book: Special deference can be shown in all continuing contacts. On matters of minor importance on which you foresee no clash of opinions, you can make a show of admiration for something he/she has done or said.

It will happen, of course, that some critics of your decision cannot be won over and cannot be mollified. Prudence then dictates that with regard to them you keep as low a profile as possible. Try to avoid any rubbing the wrong way, any unnecessary contacts, and, above all, keep them ever in mind in the formulation of other decisions in which they will have a voice.

2. WHO NEEDS TO BE INFORMED, AND HOW? Make your list no longer than the "need to know" requires—but make doubly sure that it is no smaller than that.

Translating a decision into action must be done either by others, or with the aid and compliance of others. (There are a few exceptions, e.g., a painter deciding to paint a certain landscape must do it himself. However, these are infrequent enough to be disregarded here.) Even a surgeon, who must do the operating himself, must depend upon others for make-ready, assistance, and postoperative care. Since it is so important to keep others pointed in the right direction and doing the right things, it will be well to keep in mind the following basic rules of communicating:

a. Tell *enough.*

b. Tell *clearly.* Are you using the words *few, some,* or *many* where the meaning will be better conveyed by actual numbers and percentages? (They can be rounded.) What does "nine times greater than last year's sales" mean? Does it actually mean ten times, so that this year's sales are greater by nine times? Are misunderstandings possible from the use of *percentage* rather than *percentage points*? Are you talking about profits after taxes? Or sales net of returns? Are you tuning your vocabulary to that of your readers or listeners? This is especially important where technical terms, trade jargon, or local idioms are used.

c. Tell *soon enough*. Surprise is the worst enemy of good management.

d. Tell *often enough*. Producers of TV commercials certainly practice this. In a work situation you have to steer a sure course between oversupervision and insufficient follow-up. You have to know the people you're dealing with. With a green worker, repetition must continue until both you and he know that he knows. Some matters, such as safety and quality, bear constant repetition to older and new workers alike.

e. Tell *everyone concerned*. (Cf. "need to know," Question 2, above.) Be sure that those directly involved in implementation know exactly what their duties and responsibilities are, and how they relate to the work of others. Who is going to tell them, when, and how?

f. Tell in the *right tone*. The tone of your message may be as important as the content. An effective communicator knows how to play the right variations on the tune: direct order (peremptory if need be), request (actual or camouflaged order), suggestion (actual or camouflaged order), request for volunteers (actual or camouflaged order).

g. Should the communication be *in writing*? Putting something down in writing encourages more precise thinking, to say nothing of the chaos that can ensue if too much is done off the cuff. On the other hand, most enterprises probably suffer from a glut of memos, with every memo proliferating into more memos—with recipients having to take time to dictate a reply, and to make copies for filing and later come-up, giving rise to what management expert Luther Gulick called our "carboniferous and neolithographic age."

Whether drastically to curtail all written communications must remain a matter of individual judgment. The only explicit prescription that can be offered is that before dashing off a memo you had better ask the question, *Is this memo necessary?* If it isn't, reach for the phone, walk across the hall, or take some other direct action.

3. ARE ALL BASES COVERED?

a. Check for loose ends. Have clear assignments been made so that everyone knows who is to do what, and when—and does everyone have the needed facilities so that they *can* perform?

b. Are there any weak sisters? Is realignment of key people called for, and perhaps introduction of new blood into the organization, because of need for new concepts, new techniques, and new vision? Will backstopping or extra training be required?

c. How sure are you of your key support? How well do you know the person(s) to whom you plan to assign key responsibilities?

4. IS THE DECISION (FOR THE TIME BEING AT LEAST) "CLASSIFIED"?

a. Are you sure about the real need for "classified"? If there is even the faintest odor of cover-up, you may want to reconsider the decision itself. Leaving aside, for the moment, moral imperatives, what are the chances of discovery? How seriously would your own escutcheon be smirched? Is it worth it?

b. If a "classified" status is necessary, have you arranged for proper security?

c. How shall you "answer the unanswerable"? You may be stumped for an answer because of corporate policy. Here are some guidelines:

(1) Answer straightforwardly that you can't discuss the matter because of pending legal questions, ongoing negotiations, competitive considerations, or whatever. Be as positive as you can. If the situation permits, reassure questioners that there will be no adverse effects as far as they are concerned...or, if fortunately it is the case, that all will probably stand to benefit.

(2) If possible, mention the time when full information will be made available.

(3) Determine whether certain people, because of job requirements, should be given information not made generally available. Set forth criteria they must follow regarding confidentiality.

(4) Note that there can be situations where it is better that employees *not* be given certain information even if it bears directly on their

jobs. For example, in certain inspection operations it is highly important that not even one "no-go" be allowed to pass. Security people examining luggage at an airport is a case in point. Here it is better that personnel doing the inspection do not know how statistically small is the chance of a reject getting by. Actually, the fact that the chance is so small is the very reason that it is better if they do not know it—if they were to feel that the chance is practically nil, they might relax their vigilance.

5. ARE YOU DOING A GOOD JOB OF SELLING YOUR DECISION? Practically none of your decisions will be implemented by you alone. You will have to seek authorization or permission or encouragement or cooperation or compliance or obedience. All of this calls for a *selling job*.

a. Where authorization must be secured from a higher level of management, or perhaps from an executive committee, the logic alone of what you propose will not carry the day. How you present your case can be fully as important as its substance.

At an American Management Association discussion on how to present ideas, information, facts, and programs to others, one executive made this observation:

> Marketers make a presentation with charts, colored slides, drama, proper emphasis, oral skill, and the like. But a scientist or engineer frequently stumbles along, taking an occasional glance at a scrap of paper in the palm of his hand.

No matter what area of the business you are in, you can learn from the sales and advertising departments how to improve the quality of your presentations.

6. SHOULD THERE BE PARALLEL RUNS? These are not to be confused with *pilot* runs. In a pilot run the idea is to get information as to the workability of a proposed line of action. Here we are talking about translating a final decision into action, where significant changes in habits and procedures are involved. For example, in installing or changing a computer system, it is often desirable to run the old system in parallel with the new one during a specified period under the changed operations. This idea can be adapted to many other procedural changes—for example, changes made operative in one territory or branch while others remain "as-is" for the time being.

7. HAVE YOU ARRANGED FOR FEEDBACK AND FOLLOW-THROUGH?

a. *Early warning signals*: Major General J. B. Medaris, of missile fame, summed up the management control problem in a speech before the Thirteenth National Conference on Administration of Research, as follows:

> Give me a system that will wave yellow flags in my face when I am heading into trouble, but wave these early enough for me to do something about it. What I never want you to do is to wave a *red* flag at me, so that whole projects and progress must come to a screeching stop because of some unforeseen holdup.

Major General Medaris was discussing large-scale projects and complex operations, but his words apply with equal force to anyone responsible for getting work done. Determine where "Checkpoint Charlies" should be set up, to give readings on progress or lack of progress, and to point to those responsible for slippage.

b. How good is your *upward communication?* Under Question 2 above, telling was discussed at some length. But just as important is *listening.* This is necessary in decision formulation, but it is also vital in implementation. In addition to early warning signals, you will do well to make use of key people and informal leaders in your work group. They can give you prompt and reliable feedack on attitudes, motivation, and morale. And good upward communication will give you the added bonus of ideas for improvement from people on the firing line.

8. ARE YOU ORGANIZED FOR MANAGEMENT BY EXCEPTION? Once you have set objectives and made decisions, the essence of effective management is to arrange for control reports. These are reports that indicate out-of-line conditions in ongoing operations, as distinguished from the early emergency warnings discussed above. They permit you to apply the *management by exception* principle, i.e., concentrating on trouble spots.

It is fashionable to cry out against too much paperwork. But on the other hand it is nonsense to expect timely and intelligent control without records and reports. You should ask some brass-tacks questions about the reports you routinely get that purportedly reflect the implementation of decisions you have made. Thus:

a. What is the information content of each report? Is the information *timely, accurate,* and *pertinent?*

b. Is it the sort of report that calls only for a quick glance because it is summarized in a later weekly, monthly, or quarterly report where trends will be more readily apparent?

c. Is anything in the report worth charting, so that a better cumulative and trend picture will be readily available?

d. Are the sore-thumb exceptions properly highlighted? If not, what routine procedure can be set up to get those signals from it?

e. What scheme should be set up to get the danger signals relating to your responsibilities communicated to the right spot for action as soon as possible?

9. IF A DECISION OTHER THAN THE ONE YOU ESPOUSED IS ADOPTED, WHAT SHOULD YOUR ATTITUDE AND ACTIONS BE? If the decision is in your eyes borderline dishonest, and perhaps even illegal, if it poses clear danger to workers or to the public, or if it violates your basic core of beliefs, your guideline will be as discussed in Category two, Question 12, *Whistle Blowing*.

In your ordinary business experience, few decisions in which you are involved will be of such traumatic importance to you as to be worth making an "I'd rather quit" issue out of them. If one should be that drastic, you have a problem of personal integrity on your hands. But if you are of a mind to go along, here are basic guidelines:

a. Be sure you have all the necessary facts. How will it affect your operations, and when? How final is the decision? Is this something which higher management has indicated will be reviewed after a specified time?

b. Get your lines of communication straight. If there are further questions, just how and where are the answers to be obtained? Are there to be any exceptions? Is there a procedure for possible hardship cases?

c. Be firm in calling for adherence on the part of people under your direction. Your message for key people to pass along is: "The decision has now been made. We're going to carry on under the new rules with a minimum of further palaver. Maybe at some future time the decision will be changed, but in the meantime, let's get on with our main job." But don't indicate that the matter is subject to change unless you know for sure that that is the case.

d. Don't give an indication of halfhearted support, or by a figurative shrug of the shoulders imply that management upstairs doesn't know what it is doing. Keep your own counsel.

e. Will there be hardship cases in your department? Set up individual discussions with those affected.

f. If the matter is one about which your people feel strongly, arrange for a talk with your superior, so that he or she will understand the situation. Be sure to make the point that you are going to follow through as decided—but that you want to be sure that you are doing your part in upward feedback as well as in down-the-line implementation.

g. After a suitable time lapse, make a follow-up appraisal. Are matters working themselves out? Should you change your original position? How is the general adherence in your department? Are there still some holdouts who are keeping the initial irritation alive? Are some private talks indicated?

10. ARE YOU MAKING FULL USE OF THE "INVISIBLE FORCE"? It's called "motivation" It's one of the most important distinctions between human workers and mechanical workers. You can't motivate a robot to do something "above and beyond the call of duty." You can only program it to do what it was designed to do. You can't motivate a machine: you press a button, and it's hard-wired to do what was designed into it.

There are whole libraries of books and articles on motivation, and so there is no need to belabor the points amply treated there. But it will pay to run through certain basics about the climate for motivation that will aid in implementing the decision(s) you now want to translate into action:

a. Dramatize project significance: In many operations, the significance of work in terms of results may not be obvious, and it will pay to highlight it. How far down the line can the inspiration of the end result be taken? Answer: All the way down! A young woman in a factory was gluing little pieces of wood on lever arms. A consultant making a study of the plant asked her what her job was. "Oh," she said, "I *build pianos!*"

b. Give individual recognition. This is the key which, if applied in addition to competitive wages and salaries, will unleash "latent and waiting" job enthusiasm beyond anything you may have expected. Opportunities are endless, and need hardly be catalogued here. For example, it is obvious that if a company has a cash-award system for useable suggestions, management would lose much of the effect if it privately and confidentially handed a check to an award-winning employee. The employee's reward is far more than money. He or she basks in the glory of mention in the company magazine, of a personal presentation by the big boss, of recognition at a company dinner....The reporter would give his eyeteeth for a by-line...the rising young executive wants his name on the door, the star salesman loves that prize trip to Bermuda with his wife. These are the stuff that glory is made of. No other investment in decision implementation brings bigger returns.

c. Don't skimp on praise. A sales executive made "PF" the slogan for his division. PF stands for "praise fearlessly." He said anyone who is afraid to give recognition to associates or subordinates thinks someone may advance at his expense, and is suffering from an inferiority complex.

But a point must be underscored here: With all of our emphasis on the human-relations approach, there is no intention to imply that you should abdicate your right to set goals and insist on meeting standards of quality and productivity. Sound human relations does not mean that disagreement must be avoided at all cost. Unlike the customer, the employee is not always right. When he or she is not right, he or she must be told so firmly.

But sound human relations is built on respect and consideration for the individual's feelings. An employee in tears is worth nothing to you for the rest of the day. Nor is a "slow burn" a productive source of heat. Maybe neither can be totally avoided, but they can be kept to a minimum.

d. Nervousness is contagious. Psychological insight doesn't necessarily come from majoring in psychology in college. Some people seem to be born with it, and we can all learn from them.

A cosmetics company had supplemented its eastern operations with a new plant in the Midwest. After months of quality problems, delays, and back orders, a longtime foreman in the old plant was transferred temporarily to the Midwest to help the newly recruited plant manager get things rolling. He soon had the production lines humming—and it was then that the president decided upon a drastic step. He discharged the plant manager and put the erstwhile foreman into the top job.

Shortly after this management shuffling, a consultant had occasion to visit the plant. The new "zing" in operations was immediately apparent. After a tour through the filling and packing departments with the new plant manager, they stepped into the latter's office for a chat. The plant manager had this to say: "Yes, things are rolling. But this management stuff gets me pretty nervous, even though you fellows are backing me up on paperwork. I've only been a foreman, but now the old man wants me to run the whole plant."

The consultant told him he definitely hadn't seemed nervous in the plant. "I saw you fielding questions and straightening out the problems those new employees had on the filling lines."

"Oh," was the reply, "none of the people outside would ever know I'm nervous. I have to let on that everything is under control, no matter how

I feel inside. *If I let them see I'm nervous, they will be nervous too.*"

11. ARE YOU PUTTING OBSTACLES IN YOUR OWN PATH BECAUSE YOU'RE SUFFERING FROM A "DO-IT-YOURSELF" COMPLEX? Many an executive fails to delegate, and gets so involved in *doing* that he has insufficient time for *thinking*, for keeping an eye on the big picture, and for meeting evolving situations that call for new decisions. And such close involvement in the handling of problems that should be the province of people more familiar with operating details may well lead to less than optimal implementation of the immediate decision.

If you feel that the judgmental and decision-making elements of your job are such that it is necessary for you to do most of the implementing personally, you may find it illuminating to take another look. (Review Category One, Question 12.) For every major decision there will be a host of operational subdecisions in the process of implementation. The classic prescription for the allocation of decision making in this situation is the one enunciated by Harold Smiddy, of General Electric, quoted herein in Proposition 18. (Don't look back. It's important enough to repeat here.)

> The determinant level for responsibility and authority to make a particular decision should be at the lowest organizational level where both the needed skills and competence, on the one hand, and the needed information—embracing understanding of both indirect and environmental probable impacts of the decision—on the other hand, can reasonably be brought to exist.

Two preventive measures should be kept in mind. The first is to do everything possible to avoid situations where you feel you have to jump in personally to pull chestnuts out of the fire. This involves a good job of indoctrination of new people on a job, and giving clear and complete instructions on all assignments. The second is then to avoid oversupervision. Keep in touch with what's going on, but "get off the subordinate's back" and let him or her get on with the job.

In none of the foregoing is it implied that you should abdicate the responsibility for controlling the quality of decisions made by those reporting to you. The important point to keep in mind is whether you are exercising the Smiddy form of control.

12. DO YOU HAVE A FALL-BACK POSITION? No successful general envisions defeat. In your case, having considered all factors, having made your decision and come this far to the point of implementation, you may well be sure of your ground. Nevertheless, prudence requires that you make suitable precautionary plans. Burning bridges behind you serves no constructive end. But beyond that, it will pay you to construct some serviceable additional bridges, strategically placed. No specific prescription can be offered here. However, some strategy objectives can be hazarded. Envision the worst possible scenario, and consider:

a. What would be the worst financial setback? How much of a body blow would that be? What would be the repercussions? Would it endanger other projects? What could probably be salvaged?

b. What adverse nonfinancial results would accrue? What would be the public-relations effect? What would be the effect on your personal prestige? What would probably be the duration of these adverse effects? What would be the best possible face you could put upon the story?

c. Was the decision a viable idea whose time had just not come? Should you yield, but not give up the ultimate goal, and nurture forces for a new try at a later, more propitious time?

d. What second-best alternative can be defined ahead of time? Think again about the limits of possible concessions (Category Six, Questions 6 and 7)?

13. BUT DON'T GIVE UP TOO EASILY TO THE OPPOSITION. Remember the plains of Ono. You may recall the story (Nehemiah, Ch. 6):

> He rebuilt Jerusalem's walls, and made them impregnable. His enemies, seeing they could not breach them but nevertheless hopeful of halting his work of rebuilding the city, sent repeated messengers to him, urging him to meet with them in one of the villages in the plains of Ono. But Nehemiah sent messengers back, saying "I am doing a great work and I cannot come down. Why should the work stop while I leave it and come down to you?" And he answered in this way four times.

The plains of Ono are full of people who say, "Oh no, it can't be done!" Or, "Oh no, it has been tried and failed." Or, "Oh no, it is too costly...or too dangerous...or too soon...or too late." Stay steadfast, like Nehemiah, and say, "I am doing a great work, and I cannot come down. Why should my work stop?"

Who Shall Make the Value Judgments?

War is too serious a business to be left to the generals.
                                                    —*Talleyrand*
When the main policies themselves are in need of
formulation or reformulation, then improvement of
managerial decisions which aim at implementation of
existing policies is not only useless, but often counter-
productive.   —*Y. Dror,* Design for Policy Sciences

It should be obvious that if *what shall be done, and why* is not thought through, all of the technical expertise and physical resources at your command will stand you in no good stead, and may even do you harm. They will make you more efficient, but they will not make you effective, i.e., their efficiency will simply enable you more easily to attain the wrong ends. That is why the matter of concern here has to do with policy, which should set the stage for all decision making. And policy has to do with value judgment, which, as indicated in this book's opening definitions, rests on a mental approach dictated by ingrained professional training, cultural background, moral guidelines, ethical standards, and the like.

Where shall the exercise of value judgments, the precursors of decisions and action, be centered? Who shall make the "what" and "why" decisions? Who, other than qualified specialists, *can* make them in our highly scientific and technical society?

Look at it this way:

Decisions flowing out of value judgments reflect the very *raison d'être* of an undertaking, and then continue to define and if necessary change the goals to which the undertaking is dedicated. They set the directions in which it is pointed, and provide the requisite funds and facilities, or initiate, approve, or encourage actions within the undertaking that provide or contribute to such funding and facilities.

Every undertaking is part of a larger undertaking, and the latter is part of a next higher undertaking, and so on, going up through successive hierarchical levels, until the ultimate organization unit is reached above which there are for the moment no higher hierarchies.

In the present context, *undertaking* and *organization unit* designate the same kind of entity, but the former term signifies an organization entity which is relatively short-lived, and the latter term signifies a formally structured and continuing entity, with an established place and relationships within a larger organization.

The Catholic Church is a good example of a large structure made up of smaller organization units. The total organization goes from neighborhood to parish to diocese and archbishopric on up to the See in Rome, beyond which there is no higher earthly authority—although in temporal matters it and other religious bodies are subject to the laws of the countries in which they operate. In the governmental sphere we have at the bottom level small jurisdictions as parts of regional entities, in hierarchical levels on up to the ultimate sovereign state. Above these there is at the moment no higher sovereign entity (leaving aside for the time being the still to be solidified sovereignty of the United Nations). In business, of course, there are departments and branches and divisions leading on up to subsidiary companies and finally to the parent corporate entity. Here the ultimate authority is the state and its body of laws and regulations. (In our context, "state" is itself a series of hierarchies: local, state, and federal, in the order of overriding authority.)

For every undertaking or organization unit the value judgments that justify, guide, and perpetuate it are centered in the organization unit immediately above it; and within organization units there are hierarchies or authority levels. It is important to note that the making of value judgments calls for a broad understanding and appreciation of the specialized skills, body of knowledge, expertise, and specialized products or services of the unit in question; but the decision makers in the higher unit do not necessarily share the detailed expertise in depth.

The person or group making value judgments resulting in directives to an organization unit reporting to it must view that unit in broad perspective, in terms of its relation to the goals and purposes of the larger enterprise of which it is itself a part. This value-judgment person or group cannot without loss of perspective and effectiveness immerse itself in day-by-day operations. The latter must be left to the decision maker(s) within the subordinate unit responsible for implementing the governing body's policies and directives.

For purposes of explication, let us consider the foregoing formulation under two heads: First, value judgments at the very highest level of decision: civilian direction of military operations, governmental and quasi-governmental oversight of large agencies and institutions, and boards of directors of business enterprises. Second, organization for the day-by-day operation of the functional entities subsumed under the first.

1. DECISIONS AT THE HIGHEST POLICY LEVEL. The free world now accepts without question the doctrine that the ultimate command of the military organization must rest in the hands of civilians, and here we take that as a given, deeming that it requires no further rationalizing.

Of course, the civilian government must see to it that the actual conduct of military operations is in the hands of competent military professionals, but there must be no question that the head of the civilian government can set restraints upon the extent to which military operations will be carried out. He or she can rebuke and even remove generals who go beyond instructions, or who publicly voice opposition to them—as exemplified by President Truman's summary removal of General Mac-Arthur from command in Korea in 1951. War, as General Clausewitz said, is simply the continuation of politics by other means, and only the civilian government can judge the political, economic, and home-front morale consequences of military actions, and the possible repercussions on relations with friendly and unfriendly but as yet unaligned governments.

The relationships discussed above also hold with respect to large public and quasi-public bodies, commissions, boards, and public authorities—upward, vis-à-vis the legislative or other political authority that established them, and downward vis-à-vis the designated chief operating officers who must manage the day-by-day operations. Resources are always less than the self-perceived needs of the agencies, and only the higher authority can judge priorities and allocations in the light of total social needs and fiscal constraints. Only the higher authority sees the big picture. Similarly, the boards and commissions must often scale down the budgetary requests of their chief operating officers in the light of their own larger picture of political realities and the competing needs of their agencies.

The same pattern holds with respect to corporate boards and their operating executives.

2. DECISIONS AT THE OPERATING LEVEL. The person in direct charge of an organization unit makes three kinds of decisions: (a) internal value judgment decisions having to do with the operations of the unit; (b) operational decisions regarding carrying out the work (schedules, directives, training, methods improvement, accounting controls, etc.); and (c) external value-judgment decisions resulting in policy directives to subordinate organization units.

The above model of decision-making relationships has certain organizational implications. Some examples follow.

In making a decision about the type of person who should head up a particular organization, the question to be asked first is, What are the internal/external value judgments that have to be made to ensure effective carrying out of the organization's mission? Thus where a given profession is basic to the organization's activities, the directing head should first and foremost be a respected member of that profession.

In the case of a hospital, for example, the directing head should be a professional in medicine. His (or hers) will be the burden of ultimate responsibility should something go wrong in medical treatment or surgical procedures. Those are matters on which no layperson would be qualified to make choices/decisions regarding

facilities, policies, and hiring and promotion of professional personnel. His or her's will also be the credit
for the effective carrying out of the hospital's mission
in the community and in academic medicine.

The selection procedure in determining who should
fill a vacancy in the top hospital position would logically
include a proviso that the successful candidate should in
prior professional activities have demonstrated a flair
for administration. However, that should be secondary
to medical qualifications. The governing body should
arrange for a position of deputy to the director, with
responsibility for development of budgetary procedures
and controls, personnel records, procurement and dis-
bursements, and other related business matters. But, to
repeat, the top person, the one who "calls the shots,"
should be a respected member of the medical profession.

In high-level business appointments, the same line of
reasoning applies, although there may not be the same
obvious and clear-cut professional requirement. Again,
the primary question must be as to what kind of value
judgments are paramount. These may be different at different times under differing economic and regulatory conditions. For example, are the basic problems confronting
the corporation product acceptance and marketing, or
labor relations, or manufacturing cost effectiveness and
quality, or some other concern?

In a complex organization such as a public-utility
power company, it goes without saying that a highly
important qualification of the person at the top must be
the ability to handle effectively the external value judgments that must be made regarding highly technical
organization units, such as nuclear power generation.
The latter may well be outside of his (or her) personal
expertise. However, he was presumably chosen because
he was not only highly qualified in the field of expertise
called for by the company needs at the time (which let

us say was not nuclear power), but because he was also a generalist in the sense of being able to make external value judgments about staffing and monitoring the diverse specialized areas of the company's operations. What Peter F. Drucker has said on this point, in his *The Effective Executive*, is pertinent here:

> The meaningful definition of a "generalist" is a specialist who can relate his own small area to the universe of knowledge. Maybe a few people have knowledge in more than a few small areas. But that does not make them generalists; it makes them specialists in several areas. And one can be just as bigoted in three areas as in one. The man, however, who takes responsibility for his contribution will relate his narrow area to a genuine whole.…One need not know what to do in specialized areas outside of one's own expertise, but one has a responsibility to know at least what these areas are about.

In sum, value judgments are choices/decisions made "above the confusion of the daily fray"—from a position high enough and with a vision broad enough to see the big picture.

APPENDIX A

Are You Prepared for Emergencies?

Things which you do not hope happen more frequently than things which you do hope.

—Plautus

In the steady running of an organization, the frequent need of great speed of decision is a symptom of a lack of sufficient advance thinking.

—Henry Dennison, American Industrialist

No one engulfed in an emergency will at that moment be inclined to look into a book like this one to find out what to do. But it will be useful to include here some observations on how to *avoid* emergencies and how to prepare for them when they come (and they will!).

Surprise is the worst enemy of good management. Following are some pointers bearing on Dennison's call for advance thinking. Note that steps taken in preparation for emergencies will automatically lead to the avoidance of many of them.

1. ENFORCE SAFETY AND HEALTH RULES. Certainly no further comment on this is needed.

2. HAVE STANDARD OPERATING PROCEDURES. Put them in writing and keep them up to date. Be sure everyone understands them. Occasionally there have to be exceptions to rules, but to the extent that people "go by the book," emergency situations will be avoided or alleviated.

3. HAVE CHECKLISTS. (See "Check for Loose Ends," Category Seven, 3a.)

4. PRACTICE PREVENTIVE MAINTENANCE. If you are in charge of operations calling for equipment use, make sure that "use without abuse" is stressed. Be sure maintenance as well as safety pointers are part of all written instructions and checklists on machine use. Enforce proper feeds, speeds, etc., and warm-ups if required on certain equipment before loading. Guard against overloads.

a. Keep a record of delays due to equipment failure and pinpoint and report to the maintenance department the critical places where delays and breakdowns occur frequently.

b. Have a definite schedule for periodic equipment checks, to spot potential trouble before it occurs.

Where applicable, list equipment in your operations that:

will shut down integrated operations if it fails;

is the only equipment available for its kind of job;

must be continuously available;

has a high value, calling for special care;

operates in unusually severe surroundings (Provide for care accordingly).

5. BE SURE ALL BASES ARE COVERED. Have standard backup procedures and be prepared for unexpected absences of key people. Promulgate and enforce rules regarding prior notification of absences and lateness.

6. BE SURE KEY PEOPLE UNDERSTAND THEIR FULL RESPONSIBILITIES. Do you allow sufficient authority to subordinates to handle special situations? Are key people designated to take charge in specific types of emergencies? Can they be reached at all hours? Does everyone concerned know who they are and how they can be reached?

7. DEVELOP VERSATILITY. The more people there are who know how to do more than one job, the more readily will emergencies be contained.

8. CHECK COMMUNICATION PROCEDURES. Are the affected people in your department, and in departments depending upon yours, adequately and promptly in-

formed of changes, cancellations, new priorities, and the like?

9. ON ALL NEW PROJECTS, ESTABLISH FOLLOW-UP PROCEDURES.

10. PROVIDE FOR DANGER-SIGNAL CONTROL. (See "Early Warning Signals," Category Seven, 7a.)

11. DON'T HESITATE TO DELEGATE, but keep in touch.

12. HAVE AN UNDERSTUDY. Often executives—indeed, executives all the way to the top—can't bring themselves to develop an understudy because they can't seem to face the fact that there will ever be a day when someone else will sit in their chair. Many have an abiding sense of insecurity that leads them to guard their job jealously, fearing that if they train someone to take over, that particular someone will push them out before they are ready to go. There are always good "reasons" not to develop an understudy: too busy to take the time to train a successor...no one really qualified...no rush, will definitely get around to that a bit later...would upset the morale of the department to designate a "crown prince"...and so on.

Check off these questions:

a. Who is best qualified by education, experience, and potential to handle things in your absence?

b. If there is no official "assistant-to" position under yours, can you handle the matter informally? You do not have to designate someone as your "successor," but you can let the rest of the department know whom you are holding responsible during your vacation and other absences.

c. Are there several likely candidates? Can you try them out by giving them special responsibilities for pieces of your job at certain times? Can a healthy sort of competition be developed to bring up the logical successor by natural evolution?

d. What specific guidelines have you set regarding handling matters in your absence? Are there checklists and write-ups for important procedures?

e. Can you begin "peeling off" some of the more routine parts of your job for continued handling by an understudy?

f. If there is a definitely established date for your own permanent departure—scheduled promotion, transfer, retirement, etc.—have you mapped out an orderly progression of activities for the take-over person, as an orderly program for him/her to follow during the intervening time?

13. HOLD "POST-MORTEMS." Every emergency situation or "critical incident," once weathered, should be subjected to a "post-mortem" to see what can be learned by all concerned, and to see what should be done to prevent repetition, if humanly possible. Here are some evaluation pointers:

a. Was there a breach of standard operating procedures? If not, was a blind spot in an existing procedure revealed that should be covered?

b. Was the emergency due to an equipment breakdown which could have been avoided by preventive maintenance?

c. Was this a case of panic? Did someone break down under pressure? If so, is this a personality problem or a case of inadequate training and poor supervision? Was a green employee put on a job that should have been held by a seasoned individual?

d. Does analysis reveal inadequacies or errors in communication? From you to a subordinate? From a subordinate to you? Between subordinates, or between them and other departments?

APPENDIX B

Are You Prepared for Crisis Management?

It wasn't raining when Noah built the ark.

When the flood came, Noah was ready for it. Noah's flood is the kind of crisis we are addressing now—the big, cataclysmic, overwhelming event that can threaten even the most seasoned leadership with paralyzing panic. These types of crises go several orders of magnitude beyond the kind of emergencies just discussed. Though unexpected and deplorable, they are part of the normal risks of doing business and of life in general. Going back just a few years provides a list of numbing proportions:

The nuclear power plant at Three-Mile Island, ten miles southeast of Harrisburg, Pennsylvania, March 28, 1979.

The Procter & Gamble/Rely Tampon crisis, September 1980.

The Johnson & Johnson/Tylenol crisis, fall of 1982.

The space shuttle *Challenger* tragedy, January 28, 1986.

The Chernobyl nuclear power plant disaster, eighty miles north of Kiev, April 26, 1986.

The Florida hurricane, August 24, 1992.

The World Trade Center bombing in New York, February 26, 1993.

Noah actually had an advantage over the decision makers confronted with the catastrophes listed, since he at least had ample and authoritative forewarning of what he was to prepare for. But it is now apparent that, in view of the powerful technologies being tinkered with in all parts of the globe, disasters such as those cited can strike anywhere at any time without warning.

This turn of events has spawned a new term, "megacrisis," and a new management discipline, "crisis management." The latter covers preventive steps, organizing for handling, coping when the disaster strikes, public relations, and post-mortem analysis. The American Management Association published the first comprehensive book on the discipline in 1986, *Crisis Management: Planning for the Inevitable*. The author, Steven Fink, was a member of the governor of Pennsylvania's Three Mile Island crisis-management team.

LESSONS FROM THREE MILE ISLAND AND *CHALLENGER*

Two President's Commissions were appointed to probe the Three Mile Island and *Challenger* disasters. Their recommendations provide valuable alerts on crisis management of any sort, not confined to nuclear power generation or space travel. Titles of the reports are *Report of the President's Commission on the Accident at Three Mile Island*, U.S. Government Printing Office, 1979, and *Report of the Presidential Commission on Space Shuttle* Challenger *Accident*, U.S. Government Printing Office, 1986.

The following excerpts from the TMI report highlight observations of interest to managements in general:

> As the evidence accumulated, it became clear that the fundamental problems are people related, and not equipment problems. We do not mean to limit this term to shortcomings of individual human beings—although these do exist. We mean more generally, problems with the "system" that manufactures, operates, and regulates nuclear power plants. There are structural problems in the various organization; there are deficiencies in various processes; and there is a lack of communication among key individuals and groups.

> A comprehensive system is required in which equipment and human beings are treated with equal importance.

> We note a preoccupation with regulations…. Regulations alone cannot assure safety. Indeed, once regulations become as voluminous and complex as those now in place, they can serve as a negative factor in nuclear safety…. The satisfaction of regulatory requirements is equated with safety. This commission believes that it is an absorbing concern with safety that will bring about safety—not just the meeting of narrowly prescribed and complex regulations.

> Other investigations have concluded that, while equipment failures initiated the event, the fundamental cause of the accident was "operator error." … While we agree that this statement is true, we also feel that it

does not speak to the fundamental causes of the accident. First of all, it is our conclusion that the training of TMI operators was greatly deficient. While training may have been adequate for the operation of the plant under normal circumstances, insufficient understanding, even by senior reactor operators, left them unprepared to deal with something as confusing as the circumstances in which they found themselves.

Second, we found that the specific operating procedures applicable to this accident are at the least very confusing and could be read in such a way as to lead the operators to take the incorrect actions they did.

Third, the lessons from previous accidents did not result in new, clear instructions being passed on to the operators.

In connection with the last point above, it is to be noted that a senior engineer of Babcock & Wilcox, suppliers of the nuclear steam system, found that in an earlier accident, bearing strong similarities to the one at Three Mile Island, operators had mistakenly turned off the emergency cooling system. He urged, in the strongest terms, that clear instructions be passed on to the operators. His memorandum was written thirteen months before the TMI accident, but no new instructions resulted from it.

Continuing with the commission quotes:

There is little evidence of the impact of modern information technology within the control room [even though] it might be adequate for normal operation. It is seriously deficient under accident conditions. During the first few minutes of the accident, more than 100 alarms went off, and there was no system for suppressing the unimportant signals so that operators could concentrate on the significant alarms. Overall, little attention has been paid to the interaction between human beings and machines under the rapidly changing and confusing circumstances of the accident.

Whether or not operator error "explains" this particular case, given the above deficiencies, we are convinced that an accident like Three Mile Island was eventually inevitable.

With respect to the actual handling of the emergency, the commission dealt with the questions of whether various agencies made adequate preparations for an emergency, and whether their responses were satisfactory. Its finding was negative on both questions:

> Most emergency plans rely on prompt action at the local level to initiate a needed evacuation or to take other protective action. We found an almost total lack of detailed plans in the local communities around Three Mile Island. It is one of the many ironies of this event that the most relevant planning by local authorities took place *during* the accident…. There should be a single agency that has the responsibility both for assuring that adequate planning takes place and for taking charge of the response to the emergency.

The Commission on the Space Shuttle *Challenger* Accident found glaring lapses in communication rivaling those of TMI. These communication lapses were much more disconcerting because of the possible interpretation that they were not entirely inadvertent, but dictated by a desire of a contractor to meet the wishes of its most important customer.

> The commission is troubled by what appears to be a propensity of management at Marshall [Space Flight Center, Huntsville, Alabama] to contain potentially serious problems and to attempt to resolve them internally rather than communicate them forward. This tendency is altogether at odds with the need for Marshall to function as part of a system working toward successful

flight missions, interfacing, and communicating with other parts of the system that work to the same end.

The commission concluded that the Thiokol Management [Morton Thiokol, Inc.] reversed its position and recommended the launch of 51-L, at the urging of Marshall and contrary to the views of its engineers in order to accommodate a major customer.

The commission concluded also that there was a serious flaw in the decision-making process:

A well structured and managed system emphasizing safety would have flagged the rising doubts about the solid rocket booster joint seal. Had these matters been clearly stated and emphasized in the flight readiness process, in terms of reflecting the views of most of the Thiokol engineers and at least some of the Marshall engineers, it seems likely that the launch of the 51-L might not have occurred when it did.

The waiving of launch constraints appears to have been at the expense of flight safety. There was no system that made it imperative that launch constraints and waivers of launch constraints be considered by all levels of management.

The commission found that NASA and Thiokol accepted escalating risk apparently because they "got away with it last time."

ARE YOU PREPARED FOR COPING?

The foregoing remarks highlight the kinds of things to look for and correct in order to prevent a crisis, or at least to be forewarned that a crisis of a certain nature might very well happen. While the *acute* crisis stage begins when the catastrophe actually erupts (March 28, 1979, for TMI), the crisis itself actually begins when warning signs are overlooked, or when safety rules and established operating procedures are beginning to be overlooked.

TERRORISM

Terrorism by political and criminal groups is a relatively recent and particularly virulent form of crisis. A little over a decade or so ago, terrorist attacks concentrated primarily on government facilities, diplomatic establishments, government personnel, and police. As countermeasures stiffened, the focus of attacks shifted to the more vulnerable business organizations, including in many cases the kidnapping of top-level executives.

Planning ahead should include the formation of a crisis-management team. Where terrorist kidnappings are a possibility, there should be a legally authorized executive to make decisions on ransom payments and other demands, as well as a financial officer to handle fund transactions.

For industrial organizations, an effective security system provides job-applicant background investigation, positive employee identification, visitor and vendor control, shipping and receiving area control, lighting and power equipment control, door locks and key supervision, fire and intruder alarm systems, and closed-circuit television systems.

For business offices in urban high-rise or suburban buildings, public access to executive areas should be limited structurally. Office buildings should have exterior doors that lock internally and can be monitored visually. An interior door leading to executive areas should be remotely controlled in both outer perimeters and interior areas, and, if possible, linked with law enforcement agencies. After-hours access to restrooms, offices, maintenance closets, etc., should also be strictly controlled.

An effective principle in executive protection is *keep a low public profile*. This covers primarily corporate news releases (with photographs) on promotions, transfers, awards, conference participation, travel plans, club memberships, and even social activities. Business and personal travel plans should be revealed only to those with a need to know. The pros and cons of commercial versus corporate aircraft travel should be thoroughly investigated and a corporate policy should be established.

The most anguishing decision has to do with the payment of ransom to protect the life of a kidnapping victim. No advice can be given here, beyond a strong suggestion that local, and, if in their jurisdiction, federal authorities be relied upon to handle appropriately the particular situation.

Case Example: Crisis Communications

Dow Chemical Company has produced a twenty-page "Blueprint for Crisis Communications Planning" for all location managers. This document will serve as a valuable guide for any company in any industry whose operations necessarily include catastrophic risk. With the company's permission it is described in detail here and quoted extensively.

A Blueprint for Crisis Communications Planning

INTRODUCTION

All location managers should have a written plan for handling communications in a crisis situation covering on-site or off-site incidents.

Crisis planning covers two types of events:

1. The emergency: e.g., fires, explosions, accidents, train/truck mishaps, and hurricanes.

2. The nonemergency: e.g., protests, demonstrations, release of data alleging that workers have a high rate of cancer, release of data concerning fish from a plant runoff.

These situations are news. The media, state and local government officials, and the general public have a right to know the facts as they develop. By responding quickly and honestly, you can help prevent inaccurate and false public perceptions of the incident from dominating the news stories.

The Dow policy in emergency situations is to provide news media, public officials, employees, and the general public with factual information as quickly and completely as possible.

Our objective is to develop uniform guidelines so that all Dow locations are prepared in an emergency. Crisis situations can lead to controversy, increased public scrutiny, litigation, and federal and state government intervention. If we are prepared before an emergency occurs, it will help counteract negative publicity as well as the legislative and regulatory momentum that may result.

The blueprint is designed for the person assigned to handle public relations. It is a communications plan, not an overall emergency response plan. The procedure applies if the incident is at the plant or off-site. If you need assistance in developing this blueprint, we will assign someone to work with you.

Once you have completed the blueprint, you can test its effectiveness by incorporating a media alert into one of your emergency drills. Conducting drills in advance is essential to crisis planning.

A. INTERNAL ALERT

1. The following people or their equivalents should be aware of *any* emergency. Tailor the list to your plant location. The asterisk (*) indicates priority personnel.
   (*The page provides blanks for listing names, titles, office phone, home phone, and beeper number of individuals to be notified, from Division Manager on down.*)

2. Contact Dow corporate communications staff if the emergency involves:

   multiple injuries

   any deaths

   injury to someone outside the plant fenceline

   a transportation accident where chemicals are released into the environment

   a nonemergency event that may receive national or regional publicity.

   (*This page lists names and office and home telephone numbers of certain communications personnel.*)

B. EXTERNAL ALERT

1. *Emergency Help*
   Based on the nature of the emergency, you may be in contact with the following organizations:
   (*This page provides spaces for name and phone*

number of Fire Department, Police Department, County Sheriff Department, County Health Officer, Department of Environmental Protection, Highway Patrol, and Local Hospital...with room for Other.)

2. *Media*

In an emergency you may be hearing from any of the following media representatives. A good policy is to get to know reporters in your community in advance of an emergency. You will be more comfortable in talking to them, and your credibility will be enhanced if you develop rapport beforehand.

(This page provides spaces for contact(s) and addresses and phone numbers for newspapers, wire services, television, radio, magazines, and Other.)

C. PUBLIC RELATIONS RESPONSIBILITIES

The person designated by the location manager to handle public relations in an emergency will coordinate communications activities. Depending on the type of emergency, you will need the following assistance:

Spokesperson

Serves as the media contact for the duration of the emergency. Except in special situations, no other employee will give out information to the media. All employees should be instructed to refer all questions to the spokesperson. Several articulate people should be identified in advance of a crisis. Be sure to keep a list of all media calls for follow-up purposes.

Press Escorts

Duties are to escort the media while on company grounds, coordinate arrival time with security guards, serve as couriers to relay information from the scene of the accident to headquarters, assist in writing news releases and statements, and answer telephone calls if it may be necessary to coordinate photographs as well.

Press Center Coordinator
Will be responsible for physical setup of the press center, including supplies, phone lines, and the like. Smaller locations may need to arrange an off-site facility (motel, conference center, etc.)

Communications Headquarters Coordinator
Will be responsible for physical setup of internal communications headquarters, including phone lines, supplies, food, etc.

(Space is provided for name, and office and home phone numbers.)

Transportation Coordinator
The transportation coordinator will make sure vehicles and safety equipment are available to transport media to various locations inside the gates of the facility.

(Space is provided for name and office and home phone numbers.)

Dow Personnel Identification
All personnel working on the emergency staff will wear a Dow identification badge, arm band, or hat at all times during the emergency to distinguish them from outside media, community leaders, etc.

D. BACKGROUND MATERIAL

(This section provides information on the preparation of a fact sheet on Dow and the local facility. Other sections provide detailed guidelines on Personal Injury/Death Communications Policy, Employee Relations, Community Relations, Preparation of News Releases, Spokesperson Briefing, and Press Conferences [for a major emergency].)

Index

Adler, Lee, 29
Adverse decisions,
    handling, 81–83
Allen, Fred, 59
Analysis paralysis,

Bad news, barriers
    against, 42
Balance of Nature, 62
Baruch, Bernard, 25
Bases, covered, 76–78
Basic Propositions, 3–15
Benchmarks for
    consistency, 8
Bismark, Prince Otto
    von, 29

Blocking out the
    unpalatable, 21
check list for, 68
Bluffing, 72

Catholic Church, 90
Challenger tragedy,
    104–107
Chernobyl disaster, 104
Choice, def., 1
Choice/decision process, 2
Churchill, Winston, 67
Classified information, 33
Clausewitz, General Karl
    von, 92
Cleveland, Harland, 23

Coca-Cola®, 57
Compliance with an
    opposed decision, 81
Concessions for
    compromise, 71
Conflicting aims, 61
Conscience, 9
  consequences of, 7
  consistency of, 8
  core of beliefs and, 9
Coping, 108
Credibility, 46
Credit, 65
Crisis situation, 26
Crisis communications,
    111–115
Crisis management,
    103–110
*Crisis Management:
    Planning for the
    Inevitable*, 104
  criteria for, 12
  cutoff point for, 26,
    definition, 1, D

Data gathering, 40
Decision(s), adverse
    factors influencing, 14
  blocking out the
    unpalatable, 21
  check list for, 68
  classified, 33
  by committee, 10
  conflicting, 12, 13
  conscience and, 9

consequences of, 7
consistency of, 8
core of beliefs and, 9
criteria for, 12
cutoff point for, 26
definition, 1
dilution of, 19
group, 10
half-measures in, 11, 21
intermediate, 22
irrevocable, 32
one-time vs. recurring,
    31
personal, 10
postponement of, 11
range of choice in, 29
refusal to make, 11
reversing of, 8
surrogate, 10
unworkable, 12
Dennison, Henry, 97
Descartes, 5
Devil's advocate
    technique, 70
Do-it-yourself complex,
    86
Dow Chemical
    Company, 111–115
Dror, Y., 89
Drucker, Peter F., 95

Early warning signals, 79
Ellsberg, Daniel, 34
Emergencies, 97–102
Emotional distress, 4

Epictitus, 46
Excuses, 18
Executive action, xvii;
    and quantitative
    techniques, xix
Expert opinion, 53–56
Experts, 22

Fall-back position, 87
Fallout, 57–66
Family considerations, 58
Feedback, 79
Final-decision check list,
    68
Fink, Steven, 104
Florida hurricane, 1992,
    104
Follow-through, 79
Ford, Henry, 69
Free will, 5

Gone with the Wind, 20

Halo effect, 55
Hostile influences, 73
Humane considerations,
    63

Implementation, 73–88
Information flow, 40
Insecurity, 23
Interviewing, 39
Intuition, 50–53
Irrevocable decisions, 32

James, William, 4
Johns-Manville, 57
Johnson & Johnson,
    104
Jumping to conclusions,
    46

Kernel of Consciousness,
    5

Locus of decision
    making, 14
Long-range vs.
    short-range
    consequences, 31, 58
Loss of face, 19

MacArthur, General
    Douglas, 92
Management by
    exception, 80
Management reports, 81
Management sciences, xvi
Marshaling the evidence,
    37–44
Mathematical analytical
    techniques, 3
Medaris, Major General
    J.B., 79
Mental set, 8, 12
Micawber syndrome, 19
Miller, Lawrence, 58
Minutes of meetings, 60
Moment of truth, 17–24
Moore, Geoffrey H., 49

Moral guides, 6
Motivation, 83

Need to know, 59, 74
Nervousness, 85

Objectives, 38
Ono, plains of, 88
Opinion solicitation, 41

Panic, 27
Parallel runs, 79
Pareto effect, 37
Pentagon papers, 34
Perfection, 20
Perfection, hold-up for, 43
Pilot runs, 70
Plautus, 97
Politics, 29
Post-mortems, 101
Praise, 84
Precedent, 63
Preventive maintenance, 98
Procrastination, 20
Procter & Gamble, 104
Public relations, 65, 114

Quantifying risk, 46, 48

Rationality, sentiment of, 4
Response bias in interviewing, 39
Risk, 46, 47

Roosevelt, Franklin D., 22
Rumor, 59

Sacrifices, family, 58
Satisfying, 71
Schell, Erwin H., 39
Schon, Donald A., 47
Selection, def., 1
Selling a decision, 78
Shakespeare, quoted, 73
Significant variables, 37
Sizing up, 25–35
Smiddy, Harold F., 14, 86
Suggestions, from customers, 42, from employees, 41

Talleyrand, 89
Tell techniques, 74–76
Tension and anxiety, 4
Terrorism, 109
Three-Mile Island disaster, 103, 104–108
Truman, Harry S., vi, xv, 92

Unanswerable, answers to, 77
Uncertainty, 47
Under the gun, 67–72
Understudy, 100
Unfavorable evidence, 39
Unquantifiables, 50

Upward Communication, 80

Value judgment, def., 2
Value judgments, 89–95
Wang Laboratories, 70

Weighing the evidence, 45–56
Whistle-blowing, 33
World Trade Center bombing, 104